THE BRITISH CONSTITUTION

THE BRITISH CONSTITUTION

BY

SIR IVOR JENNINGS

FIFTH EDITION

CAMBRIDGE
AT THE UNIVERSITY PRESS
1968

Published by the Syndics of the Cambridge University Press
Bentley House, P.O. Box 92, 200 Euston Road, London, N.W.1
American Branch: 32 East 57th Street, New York, N.Y. 10022

This edition © Cambridge University Press 1966

Library of Congress Catalogue Card Number: 66–15941

Standard Book Number:
521 05429 X clothbound
521 09136 5 paperback

First edition, June 1941
Reprinted 1942 1943 1944
1945 1946 1947
Second edition 1947
Third edition 1950
Reprinted 1954 1958
Fourth edition 1961
Reprinted 1966
Fifth edition 1966
Reprinted with corrections 1968

Printed in Great Britain
at the University Printing House, Cambridge
(Brooke Crutchley, University Printer)

To
L. S. E.

PREFACE

The fifth edition of a book which is going to the printers for the fourteenth time needs little explanation. The first edition was completed in 1940, during the Battle of Britain, and necessarily laid emphasis on the strains to which the British Constitution was subjected between the wars. Not much alteration was needed in 1946. Though the preface was written in Ceylon, most of the amendments were made in England in 1945, just about the time when the first Labour Government with a majority came into power, and it was impossible to guess what changes the Constitution would exhibit in the post-war world. Some of these changes were evident in 1949, when I had the good fortune to be able to prepare a new edition while I was the guest of the President and Fellows of Magdalen College, Oxford. Most of the alterations then made in the book seem to have stood the test of the experience of ten years.

Many more alterations had to be made in the fourth edition. The events of 1919–39 were no longer familiar to the younger readers, and I tried to substitute more modern examples, though this was not always possible because frequently there were none. In the process of amendment I tried to meet the needs of readers overseas, who seemed to be numerous, and who might not know much of British History. The greatest changes were made in the sections dealing with parties and elections. While the rest of the book was based mainly on *Cabinet Government* and *Parliament*, these sections were based upon the preliminary studies for *Party Politics*, which has now been published. Not only has my own research been more extensive, but also others, notably at Nuffield College, Oxford, the London School of Economics, and the Universities of Manchester and Bristol, have produced valuable election studies. Also, modern elections are fought with the aid of public opinion polls, broadcasting and television, with considerable effect not only on the technique of electioneering but also on the attitudes of the parties. These sections have therefore been rewritten and appropriate amendments made elsewhere. I hope that the book now gives a picture of the British Constitution as it was at the end of 1964.

W. I. J.

Trinity Hall, Cambridge
February 1965

PUBLISHER'S NOTE

Sir Ivor Jennings completed his work on the revision of this book for the fifth edition shortly before his death.

CONTENTS

CONTENTS

PLATES

CHAPTER I

GOVERNMENT BY THE PEOPLE

1. WE, THE PEOPLE

In one of the least prudent of his speeches, Joseph Chamberlain used a phrase which has become historic. He was defending the proposals of the Unionist Government, opposed by the Liberals, for additional grants to members of the Royal Family. That in itself was enough to anger the Liberals, for Joseph Chamberlain the Unionist was now supporting what Joseph Chamberlain the Radical had opposed before he had changed sides in 1885. Stung by Opposition taunts, he jeered at 'honourable members who profess on all occasions to speak for the People with a capital P'. He went on to say: 'These honourable members tell us it is a shameful thing to fawn upon a monarch. So it is; but it is a more shameful thing to truckle to a multitude.' Truckle to a multitude? The Liberal party was not likely to forget that phrase and there must have been hundreds of platforms from which Liberal speakers for the next decade reminded 'the People with a capital P' what Joseph Chamberlain thought of them.

In doing so they were falsifying his character. Chamberlain more than any Unionist statesman of the late nineteenth century except perhaps Lord Randolph Churchill recognised the need to bow to public opinion—to truckle to the multitude. He had come into national politics at the head of a popular movement in Birmingham; he had inspired the 'Radical Programme' of 1884 because he believed that the people wanted something more positive than the Liberal leaders were offering them; later on, he restrained Lord Milner's ardour for war against the Transvaal until he was

1

sure that the larger section of public opinion had been convinced of the inevitability of a conflict; and one of the reasons for his raising the banner of 'tariff reform' after 1900 was his belief that the Unionists, who had snatched a majority in the 'khaki election' at the end of the Boer War, would be heavily defeated next time if they did not capture the electors' imagination. That he proved to be wrong in his choice of remedy does not prove that his diagnosis was faulty.

In this respect Chamberlain was more in tune with the spirit of the Constitution after the franchise reform of 1884 than any of the leaders of the Liberal party. He was also far more the democratic politician than the retiring and unapproachable Lord Salisbury, who led the Unionist parties. He realised that the Constitution had become democratic and that the public opinion with which ministers were concerned was now represented not by the gossip of the clubs of Pall Mall but by the opinions of workers in the factories of Birmingham and the mines of South Wales. Essentially the task of a politician was to persuade the 'People with a capital P' to give him and his policies their support.

The most obvious reason for the change was the progressive extension of the franchise. People who have the vote have to be persuaded. It must be remembered, however, that the process of persuasion can be intelligent only if the people are enlightened. If they are so ignorant of political problems that they can be stampeded by slogans or specious promises or allegations of unknown terrors, or if they do not see that acquiescence in corrupt government is to take part in a conspiracy to establish tyranny, a wide franchise is an invitation either to corrupt demagogy or to nationalist dictatorship. It would be easy to produce examples from other countries. When this book was first written twenty-five years ago, some of the most cultured peoples of Europe were governed by foul dictatorships; and since then many peoples have tried democracy but failed to work it. In Great Britain, this problem has never attained considerable proportions because the franchise in fact lagged behind political education, and the difficulty has been that whole sections of the population capable of taking part in democratic government have until recently been excluded from it. Indeed, the extension of the franchise has coincided with a gradual cleaning up of the corruption which prevailed in the eighteenth century, though both had a common cause, the political education of the middle classes.

It is not too much to say that, in Great Britain, government by opinion, or 'truckling to a multitude', arose because of the extension of political education rather than because of the extension of the franchise. A vocal opinion can mould policy even where it cannot be expressed on the hustings or in the ballot box. For instance, nothing could be more unrepresentative than the so-called representative system in Scotland between the Union in 1707 and the first Reform Act in 1832. The Scottish members of the House of Commons were chosen by corrupt oligarchies, usually under the control of the Government. Accordingly, the Government had the forty-five Scottish members in its pocket. Since the Government was chosen by reason of the balance in the House of Commons, where the English element was dominant, it might be assumed that in the eighteenth century the inevitable consequence of the Scottish franchise (laid down, be it noted, by the Scottish Parliament before its demise) was a permanent injustice to Scotland. The contrary was the case because, though the Scottish members were always 'King's friends', supporters of the Government, they were also Scots. The price of their continued allegiance was justice to Scotland. It was not they, however, who determined what was justice to Scotland, but the vocal opinion of Scotland: and this was very wide, because the Presbyterian system in the Kirk had taught large numbers of the Scottish people to argue about and take part in the consideration of public questions, and generally the educational system (under the influence of the Kirk) was far better in Scotland than in England (where the Church was then

3

antagonistic to education and was itself a close oligarchy). The Scottish artisan, for instance, had influence on British policy in relation to Scotland long before the English artisan had much influence on British policy in relation to England.

Nevertheless, there were signs towards the end of the century that even in England a wider political education was developing. The younger Pitt won his first election in 1784 not merely because all the electioneering resources of the Crown were placed at his disposal (including the forty-five Scottish seats), but also because the spectacle of the great Earl of Chatham's son defying a corrupt parliamentary majority appealed to the middle classes, enfranchised and unenfranchised alike. Wilberforce deliberately appealed to the 'conscience' of the unenfranchised middle classes in order to force the abolition of the slave trade through a Parliament in which the West India interest was strong. The Whigs were induced to adopt electoral reform in 1830 simply because there was a vocal public opinion which demanded it. Cobden and Bright, in their attack on the Corn Laws, went even further. They appealed to the working classes, who were still not enfranchised but who were beginning to have opinions of their own, with the result that, in time of famine, a majority for repealing the Corn Laws was found in a Parliament most of whose members had been elected to maintain them. The explanation of these and many other examples is that no person ever thinks out public policies from first principles. He does not collect all the literature from Plato and Aristotle onwards in order to find out whether there should be a limitation of the hours of work in a factory. The member for a borough which had come under the influence of a landowner was, of course, concerned primarily with the opinions of his patron; but both patron and member had their opinions formed for them by contact with others. What was said in the tap-room in the county town was of far more direct importance than anything said in Adam Smith's *Wealth of Nations*; though something of what Adam Smith said became the talk of

4

the saloon bar when the price of wheat went rocketing upwards.

When a large section of opinion becomes politically conscious it begins to demand the franchise as a right. Soon the opinion prevails, as it prevailed in 1832, that an extension of the right to vote is necessary. If at that time a political party thinks that it can secure advantage by adopting the public opinion as its own, the result will be a Reform Act, again as in 1832. Nevertheless, the immediate result of such an Act is not very great. None of the franchise reforms of the nineteenth century produced an immediate change in the character of the membership of the House of Commons or in the policies of parties. If the balance of power is shifted, as it was in 1832 and 1867, there are ultimate effects, though they are incalculable because opinion is shifting at the same time. The importance of the changes in the franchise has, however, been overemphasised. It was at least equally important that throughout the nineteenth century the middle classes were becoming politically more responsible and the working classes were becoming politically conscious. Education in the academic sense was spread very slowly, partly of course because the middle-class oligarchy felt that education was dangerous to its political supremacy—it is one of the difficulties of the extension of democracy that democracy cannot extend without education and that it is difficult for education to extend without democracy. More important, however, is the fact that what may be called political education developed ahead of academic education. Political education is possible even among an illiterate population. The critical discussions in presbyteries was probably more important than the direct educational activities of the Presbyterian Kirk. In England and Wales the work of the schools maintained by the religious bodies began to spread downwards, though it never went very far or very deep until the State assumed a measure of responsibility after 1870. More was done, in fact, by the very practical training obtained in mechanics' institutes, the working-men's clubs, the trade unions and the co-operative societies. The effect of these influences was cumulative, because ordinary social inter-course is the most fruitful means for the spread of ideas. Perhaps the Anti-Corn Law League addressed only a minority of the population, but its ideas spread around the factories and were the common talk of the pubs. The cotton operative who could read what Disraeli said about Gladstone was the source of information, no doubt garbled, for a dozen.

Universal education, a popular press, broadcasting and television have now provided Great Britain with what is, comparatively, an instructed electorate. It is true that few electors have any expert knowledge of anything outside their own jobs: but this is as noticeable in the college common-room as it is in the factory. Nor has our educational system given equal opportunities to all classes, though it has gone very far in that direction. What is needed, however, is not so much knowledge as plain common sense, the ability to seize the point of an argument when it is presented in an ele-mentary fashion. If the State had to decide nice points in the theory of knowledge or consider the composition of matter, it could do no more than leave the question to its philosophers and scientists. Fortunately, the general questions of public policy are not of this order, and for those aspects of it, such as the precise relationship between a currency and its gold backing, which are, the ordinary individual usually has enough sense to rely on the experts. There is of course a possibility that attractive and specious arguments on tech-nical matters—such as the nature of credit—will induce the common man to override the expert in the expert's own field; but, generally, the ordinary man will not listen to a compli-cated argument, and he is more concerned with the ends than the means.

Nor must it be thought that public opinion considers policy from a wholly detached and impartial angle. The ordinary

6

individual is concerned with the general tendency as it affects himself, his family and his friends. He soon discovers that he has an interest in the welfare of the community as a whole, and in any case there is a mass of sentiment which induces altruism. The income-tax payer may rush to pay his tax because he thinks that the interest of the community requires it; the old age pensioner may send a shilling to the Chancellor of the Exchequer. Volunteers for the public service, at considerable loss and inconvenience to themselves, can always be obtained. Similarly, the individual considers the welfare of the community when he casts his vote: but he considers it in the background of his own interests. The landowner thought that the Corn Laws provided the backbone of the State, while the industrialist considered that they hindered the increase in the national income and, of course, in his own. In the last resort, most people are prepared to sacrifice their own interest for that of the community; but often they see no reason why they should not gain what they can, and perhaps even more often they assume that their interest and the interest of the community are one. It is to be expected that a business man will object to the transfer of his profitable business to the State, though it is not inevitable that he should object to the transfer of other businesses—for instance, the banking business. It is equally to be expected that the worker should be anxious for higher wage rates and better conditions in his own trade, though not necessarily in other trades— because the effect may be to increase the cost of living. In practice, however, business men combine in trade associations for their mutual protection, and workers combine in trade unions for their mutual protection. This being the dominant conflict of opinion in ordinary times, the result is shown in the support of different political parties. The alignment is never precise, however; and, in particular, not all the workers are agreed that the policy of the Labour party is that best suited to the interests of themselves and other people. In addition, there is a large and growing body of individuals

7

outside the two main interest groups, sometimes moving in one way and sometimes in another.

Nor must this or any other cause necessarily produce irreconcilable opposition. Great Britain is a small island with a very homogeneous population. Few think of themselves primarily as English, Scots or Welsh. The sting has long ago been taken out of religious controversy. The population is so closely interdependent that there is little economic agitation on a regional basis, as there sometimes is in a large country like the United States. There are class divisions and (what is often the same thing) economic divisions, but they are not wide or deep, and they are tending to disappear through heavy taxation at the one end and high wage rates at the other. We are a closely-knit economic unit, with a large measure of common interests and a long patriotic tradition. The density of the population gives Britain one of the best systems of communication in the world. The British Broadcasting Corporation provides the news while we shave; a London newspaper can be read at breakfast in the West or the North, in Wales or in Scotland. It is not uncommon for one-fifth of the whole population to see the same television programme at the same time. Consequently, the elements of agreement are much more numerous and important than the elements of disagreement. There is always a common public opinion which has agreed about principles, and the divergencies are more often about methods than about objects.

It is, nevertheless, over these differences that political debate ranges. The Constitution must provide some means for their resolution. The classic theory of democracy assumes that, because the differences are in the main the consequences of divergences in individual interest, the only way to resolve them is to take the majority opinion. The argument need not be based on 'the greatest happiness of the greatest number'. The intelligent individual realises that the whole is greater than the part, and that the majority gains more from the collaboration of the minority than from its suppression.

Moreover majorities become minorities and, if there is a tradition of suppression, become the victims of tyranny in their turn. What is asserted is that one man's opinions on public policy is no better than another's. The expert knows only a little about something, and is no more entitled to decide a general policy than any other person.

This is the argument for the principle of 'one man (or woman), one vote'. It was not fully carried out until 1948, when the university constituencies were abolished and the right of a person to vote in a constituency in which he had a 'business premises qualification' but did not reside was taken away. The law is now very simple: 'The persons entitled to vote...in any constituency shall be those resident there on the qualifying date, who, on that date and on the date of the poll, are British subjects of full age and not subject to any legal incapacity to vote.'

2. THE PEOPLE'S CHOICE

A wide franchise is not the sole test of democracy. Everything depends on how and for whom the electors are allowed to vote. The cardinal factors of British democracy are that the character of the British Government depends essentially on the results of the last general election, that there must be a general election at least once every five years (except in war-time), and that the electors have a choice exercised freely and secretly between rival candidates advocating rival policies. These facts are significant in themselves; they differentiate British democracy from the so-called 'people's democracy' of the communist countries and from the autocratic systems of other authoritarian states. They are even more important in their consequences. The Government stands or falls by the result of a general election. Every member of the House of Commons must seek re-election in not more than five years. Every action of the Government is done with close attention to the movements of public opinion in the country at large, and every time a member of Parliament casts a vote in the House of Commons he considers the movement of opinion in his own constituency. Nor is this all; the general election produces not only a Government but also an Opposition. Facing the Prime Minister is the Leader of the Opposition; opposite the Treasury Bench, where sit the members of Her Majesty's Government, is the Front Opposition Bench, where sit the leaders of Her Majesty's Opposition. The Leader of the Opposition is the alternative Prime Minister; only a slight shift in public opinion is necessary to give Her Majesty's Opposition a majority in the House and so to convert them into Her Majesty's Government. The result is to make the Government and the House very sensitive to public opinion. We have government by the people not merely because the people exercises a choice freely and secretly at short intervals, but also because it follows from the fact that the whole machinery of government—the House of Lords is a very minor exception—is keyed to public opinion. This fact will become more apparent as our exposition proceeds. For the present it is necessary to examine this popular choice, to find out how real and effective it is.

There must be a general election at least once every five years, because the law so provides. From 1715 to 1911 the maximum duration of Parliament was fixed at seven years. When the powers of the House of Lords were reduced in 1911, however, the maximum duration of Parliament was reduced to five years, because it was thought that, the effective powers of the House of Commons having increased, the majority ought to secure a renewal of its 'mandate' more frequently. This rule is, however, a rule of law; and like every other rule of law it can be altered by Parliament. Unlike other rules of law, however, it cannot be altered by the House of Commons alone, because the Parliament Acts, which enable the House of Commons to overrule the House of Lords after a delay of one year, specifically except laws extending the maximum duration of Parliament. Such a law therefore needs the consent of the House of Lords as well as the House of Commons. In the House of Lords the Conservative party has a large permanent majority. Consequently, a Labour or Liberal Government with a majority in the House of Commons cannot extend the duration of Parliament without the consent of the Conservative Opposition. A Conservative Government with a majority in the House of Commons, or a Coalition Government supported by the Conservative party, would be in a more dangerous position. It would be politically dangerous, however, to pass such a law without a very good reason. Unless it had the mass of the electors behind it, the Government would present a valuable propaganda weapon to the Opposition. Some of its supporters in the House of Commons might vote against it, and it would probably lose seats at by-elections. Even if it maintained its majority during that Parliament, its 'unconstitutional' action would be one of the great arguments against it when ultimately the general election arrived, and it is possible that it would then be almost annihilated by the electors.

The British Constitution provides no check against a Conservative Government which really intended to go 'authoritarian', because a Government which had majorities in both Houses could do what it pleased through its control of the absolute authority of Parliament. It is possible that the Queen might intervene and exercise some of her dormant legal powers. Subject to this, we always run the risk, because we have no written Constitution limiting the power of Parliament. Even a written Constitution, however, is but a slight check—as many dictators have shown—and the foundation of our democratic system rests not so much on laws as on the intention of the British people to resist by all the means in its power attacks upon the liberties which it has won.

In fact, the duration of an existing Parliament has been extended only in extreme conditions. The Parliament of 1715, which was due to expire in 1718 under the Triennial Act of

11

1694, prolonged its own existence to a maximum of seven years because the Jacobite Rebellion had only just been put down, and it was feared that the conditions necessary for a free election might not be obtained. The Bill was strenuously opposed by the Opposition, but there appears to have been little opposition in the country. In any case, the conditions of to-day, under a democratic franchise, are very different. The Parliament of 1911, which was due to expire in January 1915, prolonged its life by a series of annual Acts until 1919—though it was eventually dissolved in November 1918—because of the conditions of war. There was then a Coalition Government in office with the support of the three main parties, and there was no effective opposition to it in either House. The Parliament of 1935 was continued from 1940 to 1945 by annual Acts and so became the longest Parliament since the seventeenth century. Again there was war and again a Coalition Government representing all parties.

The Parliament Act fixes the maximum duration of Parliament at five years. It does not provide that a Parliament must last for so long. The Queen, who for this purpose invariably—or almost invariably—acts on the advice of the Prime Minister, may dissolve Parliament at any time. Elections are usually held more frequently than every five years. Not only does a Government defeated in the House of Commons, like the Labour Government of 1924, normally appeal to the people, but so does a new Government formed as a result of internal dissensions—such as the Conservative Government formed in 1922 through the decision of Conservative members to withdraw support from Lloyd George's Coalition Government, and the National Government formed in 1931 after the resignation of the Labour Government. Moreover, a Government which desires to set out upon a new policy will and ought to appeal for a 'mandate', as Mr Baldwin appealed for a mandate for protective tariffs in 1923. Again, a Government with a small majority, like the Labour Government of 1951, may want to end its precarious position. Finally, a Government naturally chooses the moment for an election most favourable to its own prospects. If it allows Parliament to expire, it may have to conduct its electioneering while it is passing through a period of temporary unpopularity. Consequently, Parliament is usually dissolved well before the expiration of its normal life. For these reasons, during the twenty years' peace between 1918 and 1939, we had not five elections but seven; and between 1945 and 1964 there were not four elections but six.

Theoretically, the elector votes not for a Government but for a member of Parliament. Until 1832 the House of Commons represented in theory the counties and boroughs or, in Scotland, the burghs. Though there were exceptions, most of them had two members and each elector had two votes. As democratic ideas developed in the nineteenth century this arrangement, which paid no attention to size of electorate or population, was considered to be unfair, and so the Reform Act of 1832 enfranchised some large towns which were not boroughs, disfranchised some towns which were boroughs, and gave one seat only to some of the smaller towns. In 1868 there was an even larger measure of 're-distribution', and in 1885 the theory of the representation of 'communities' was in large measure given up, by dividing the counties and larger boroughs into single-member constituencies. There were still some exceptions, because boroughs which had two members both before and after 1885 remained as two-member constituencies in which each elector had two votes. If they still had two seats in 1918 they remained two-member constituencies even after the re-distribution then effected; and it was only after 1948 that the principle of 'one man, one vote, one value' was consistently and completely applied.

The change was so long delayed not only because of the innate conservatism of English political institutions but also because there was a case for representation of 'communities'. To take an example at random, a constituency which consists

of 'the Bablake, Foleshill, Holbrook, Radford and Sher-
bourne wards of the county borough of Coventry', is really
not an entity at all. It has no justification for being represented in Parliament. It is simply a convenient collection of
people for getting a member elected. On the other hand,
Coventry as a whole is a social, economic and (we hope)
cultural unit, with peculiar characteristics which ought to be
represented in Parliament. The weakness of this argument is,
however, twofold. First, it is no longer true that our towns
and counties are represented in Parliament as entities, or
would be if they were not divided. Our problems are national
problems and any member who kept talking about Coventry
would be a bore. The members who represent Coventry may
never have lived there; perhaps one or two of them (privately)
would express the view that there were few places less attractive than Coventry. To be sent to represent Coventry is no
doubt an honour, but the member's primary purpose is not to
represent Coventry but to vote according to his conscience,
his party, or his chances of getting re-elected. As Lord
Coke said more than three hundred years ago, though he is
elected for his constituency he 'serveth for the whole realm'.
He helps to decide national policies on national grounds;
he is not a representative of a 'community', supporting
local interests or a local patriotism; he does not take instructions from his constituents, though he runs the risk of losing
their support if he disagrees with them too thoroughly; he
need not be, and probably is not, a local resident.

Secondly, as party politics developed on modern lines it
was seen that the multi-member constituency was unfair. If
a two-member constituency contains 45,000 Whigs and
35,000 Tories and if each elector casts two votes on party
lines the constituency will return two Whigs. If it is divided
into two constituencies, one of which contains 25,000 Whigs
and 10,000 Tories, while the other contains 20,000 Whigs and
25,000 Tories, it will return one Whig and one Tory. Nor is
this a fanciful example for many of our towns have areas

which are socially and economically and therefore politically differentiated. It used to be said, with conscious exaggeration, that the Conservatives were to windward of the Liberals, because the residential areas are to windward of the factories, and it is still true in most cities that the West End is Conservative. If, however, our example of a two-member constituency were typical the Tories could never win a single seat unless they captured 5,000 Whig votes, and then they would win two seats.

The example shows the importance of 'distribution'. It also shows how unlikely it is that parties will agree either on the principle or on the practice. Some countries, in fact, have a tradition of 'gerrymandering', which includes not only distributing seats so as to favour the party in power but also drawing boundaries so as to win seats. The example given above may be taken to illustrate this problem. If there are 45,000 Whigs and 35,000 Tories, the Tories are mostly in the West End, and the town is divided by a line drawn north and south, it will return one Whig and one Tory. If, however, the same town is divided by a line drawn east and west it will return two Whigs.

It says much for the gentlemanly character of British politics that an attempt it usually made to secure agreement, though it must be added that most party managers take care not to be too compromising. In 1918 there was a Coalition Government in office and redistribution was effected by agreement, the boundaries being drawn by commissioners presided over by Mr Speaker. In 1944 there was again a Coalition Government, which produced both a short-term plan (which was carried out in 1945) and a long-term plan. The long-term plan was modified by the Labour Government, which was accordingly accused by the Opposition of gerrymandering. Both in 1944 and in 1948, however, the boundaries were drawn by commissions. Also, the law now contains permanent provision for commissions, presided over by judges, whose task is to redistribute seats at intervals

15

of not less than ten years nor more than fifteen years. The number of seats for Northern Ireland is fixed at 12, and the number for Great Britain is to be not substantially greater or less than 613, of which not less than 71 are to represent Scotland and not less than 35 are to represent Wales. Accordingly, the House of Commons will be kept at approximately 625, and changes will be made as population shifts. There have in fact been 630 seats since 1955, thus providing a very large House, manageable because of the party system.

The single-member constituency has the advantage that it is comparatively small and enables the member to establish personal contact with large numbers of his constituents. They feel that he is their member, and he feels a personal responsibility for their welfare. It is, however, fallacious to assume that normally the electors vote for an individual. Very few of them know anything about the candidates except their party labels. The British political system differs from many other systems in that the local member is rarely the 'favourite son' of the constituency. The nineteenth century used to speak of 'carpet-bagger' candidates—candidates who came down to the constituency with their 'carpet-bags' at the beginning of the campaign, put up at the local hostelry for a few weeks, and then went back either cheerfully to Westminster or dolefully whence they came. The term has dropped out of use, not only because carpet bags are no longer seen, but also because nearly all candidates are carpet-baggers. They have been chosen by local political associations, but the associations are branches of national parties, and their main concern is to choose 'good party men' who will support the national party in Parliament. If a suitable candidate is available locally, so much the better; but almost invariably he has to compete for the nomination with strong candidates from elsewhere. It is true that a Welsh constituency insists upon a Welshman, and that many Scottish constituencies insist on Scotsmen. It does not often happen, however, that Muddleton is represented by a Muddletonian. The elector does not

16

look round among his acquaintances to find out which of them is best capable of representing him in Parliament. He learns his politics in political discussion at home, in the factory, in the club; he reads the newspaper which gives him the best racing tips or which panders to his other (or his wife's) tastes, and comes to conclusions about prominent politicians and their policies from the news which it gives; he listens to the political leaders on the wireless and studies them on television; and he then decides which party (if any) shall receive his support.

The qualities of the candidate therefore have little to do with his vote. A very good candidate may pick up a few hundred votes by assiduous 'nursing'. If by chance a prominent Muddletonian does get selected, he may obtain even a thousand votes which are cast for him and not for his party. A courtesy peer who has a handsome or gracious wife may be able to capitalise the snobbery of the back streets. These factors may prove important in a few constituencies, but generally speaking it is the party label that matters. This statement can be proved not merely by common experience, but also by sampling enquiries in the constituencies and by analysis of the voting in the double-member constituencies which existed before 1948. Brighton, for instance, was represented by two members, and each of its electors had two votes. It may be assumed that one of the two Conservatives was more able, more popular, more persuasive than the other. Accordingly, if the electors voted for the man rather than for the party, there ought to be a substantial difference in the votes cast for the two candidates. Actually, we find that (with rare exceptions) the two Conservatives, the two Liberals and the two Labour candidates in any double-member constituency were within a couple of hundred votes of each other. That is to say, the electors had made up their minds according to the policies of the parties, and not according to the personalities of the candidates. In the great majority of constituencies personality is irrelevant. The representation of a 'safe seat' is determined by the choice of the local party association. The representation of the more doubtful constituencies is determined by two factors only, the general balance of political opinion, and the choice of the local party association. In almost all cases it is the label and not the candidate that matters.

The consequences are important. For instance, it places a very great public responsibility upon the local party associations. For our present purpose, however, the point of interest is that the situation minimises the value of the single-member constituency. The real purpose of the election is not to give Muddleton a representative, but to enable all the Muddletons together to choose a Government by choosing a majority in the House of Commons. Individuals in Muddleton want some representative to put their special complaints to ministers—John Smith wants to know why he has not had a pension; Herbert Thomas thinks that 'the means test man' has not given him a large enough allowance; the Chamber of Commerce wants a late delivery of letters; the local trades council thinks that some assistance should be given to local industry—but any active member can do this, and he need know very little about Muddleton. What is important is that the single-member constituencies shall produce the right balance of political forces. Actually, this is just what they sometimes fail to do.

In the first place, the minority in a constituency is completely unrepresented, except so far as the electors of that party secure majorities in other constituencies. For instance, in Somersetshire (including Bath) in 1966 the Conservative party won all seven seats with a total poll of 162,000, whereas the Labour party, with a total poll of 135,000, won no seat at all. This would be intolerable if Somersetshire were a separate 'community', with ideas and aspirations of its own. In fact, however, the Labour voters of Somersetshire were represented by the Labour members elected elsewhere. In County Durham (including the borough), for instance, the boot was on the other foot. The Labour party won all eighteen seats with a total poll of 500,000, whereas the

Conservative party, with a total poll of 234,000, won no seats.

The homogeneity of British politics thus helps to cancel out the oddities of representation through single-member constituencies. That it does not do so entirely is shown by the differences in the percentage of votes cast for the two major parties and the percentages of seats won by them in elections from 1945.

	Conservative		Labour	
	votes	seats	votes	seats
	%	%	%	%
1945	40·0	33·3	48·0	61·4
1950	43·5	47·7	46·1	50·4
1951	48·0	51·3	48·8	47·2
1955	49·7	54·8	46·4	44·0
1959	49·4	58·1	43·8	41·0
1964	43·4	48·1	44·1	50·3
1966	41·9	40·1	47·9	57·6

These oddities are even more noticeable when the figures for smaller parties, which cannot put up candidates in all, or nearly all, constituencies, are considered. For instance, the Liberal party had 311 candidates nominated in 1966, and they obtained 2,328,000 votes but only twelve seats.

This, however, introduces another point. What causes the oddities is not merely the system of single-member constituencies, but also the fact that in many constituencies there are not two candidates, but three or even more. While the Conservative party, or the Labour party, may hope to make up on the swings what it loses on the roundabouts, a minority party like the Liberal party can not. It could, in theory, have one-third of all the votes cast and yet not gain a single seat, because in every constituency either the Conservative or the Labour candidate might be 'first past the post'. This is theoretical, because if it were so strong there would almost certainly be local party compacts in which the local Conservative (or Labour) party would withdraw its candidate in one constituency in order to get Liberal support in another constituency and so to defeat the Labour (or Conservative) candidate. It is nevertheless true that, since 1918, the

Liberal party has been much stronger among the electorate than it has been in the House of Commons.

The consequence is that representation in the House of Commons may give a distorted picture of the state of opinion in the country. The general impression which most people had of the general election in 1918, for instance, was that Mr Lloyd George's Coalition swept the country with such slogans as 'Hang the Kaiser', 'Make Germany Pay', and 'A Land fit for Heroes to live in'. The Coalition Government had 525 supporters in the House of Commons, while Opposition parties had 181 (including 73 from the Sinn Fein party, which was over-represented). If each party had been represented proportionately, however, the Government would have had 395 supporters and the Opposition 311 supporters. The actual majority for making Germany pay, and the rest, was 344; it ought to have been 84. It is possible to assert, and it has been asserted, that the Treaty of Versailles would have been very different if Mr Lloyd George had not had so many 'hard-faced men' watching his every movement and protesting vehemently at every suggestion of clemency to the defeated enemy.

This is a serious accusation, and one which could not have been made so strongly if the previous Parliament had not rejected certain of the proposals of the Speaker's Conference on whose main recommendations the new franchise laws of 1918 were based. The Conference had agreed that in every single-member constituency the alternative vote should be used. This meant that the elector, instead of plumping for one candidate by putting a cross against his name, would place the candidates in order of preference. If no candidate secured an absolute majority, the first preferences given for the lowest candidate would be ignored, and the second preferences distributed. Suppose, for instance, that in counting the first preferences the following result had been obtained:

Cholmondeley (Co.Un.)	25,000
Cadbury (Lib.)	20,000
Jones (Lab.)	15,000

We may assume that most of the Labour voters had given the

The Cabinet room, No. 10 Downing Street

Liberal candidate as their second choice; but suppose that 2000 had chosen the Coalition-Unionist and 3000 had not given a second choice at all. The result would then be:

Cadbury (Lib.)	30,000
Cholmondeley (Co.Un.)	27,000

This result is alleged to be fairer, because a majority of the electors preferred the Liberal to the Coalition candidate.

In addition, the Speaker's Conference proposed that large towns with more than two representatives should be formed into single constituencies, and that voting should be based on the principle of proportional representation by the single transferable vote. As in the case of the alternative vote, each voter would mark the candidates in order of preference. The difference is, however, that whereas under the alternative vote system each voter has one vote for one member, under proportional representation there would be at least three members, and each elector would have only one vote, which would be transferred in the order of his preferences.

Let us suppose that a town which, under a single-member system, would have returned three Coalition candidates had formed a single constituency under proportional representation. The first preferences might be divided as follows:

First Count

Cholmondeley (Co.Un.)	85,000
Cadbury (Lib.)	65,000
Berkeyley (Co.Lib.)	50,000
Jones (Lab.)	45,000
Fry (Lib.)	20,000
Chamberlain (Co.Un.)	15,000
	280,000

Three members have to be elected; and there are 280,000 votes. If any candidate receives 70,001 votes he *must* be elected, because $3 \times 70,001 = 210,003$. The fourth candidate would thus have at most 69,997 votes. Accordingly, Cholmondeley has 14,999 votes to spare, and if we want to give equal value to every vote, we must divide this surplus among the other candidates. Taking now Cholmondeley's *second* preferences, we

Counting the votes

find them divided among the other candidates in a certain proportion. Dividing 14,999[1] votes in that proportion, we reach the following:

Second Count

Cholmondeley (Co.Un.)		70,001
Cadbury (Lib.)	65,000 + 200	= 65,200
Berkeley (Co.Lib.)	50,000 + 1000	= 51,000
Jones (Lab.)	45,000 + 100	= 45,100
Chamberlain (Co.Un.)	15,000 + 13,599	= 28,599
Fry (Lib.)	20,000 + 100	= 20,100
		280,000

On this second count, no candidate except Cholmondeley gets 70,001, so we must take the bottom candidate and divide up his second preferences (or the third preferences of the 100 people who voted for Cholmondeley first and Fry second). The result is as follows:

Third Count

Cholmondeley (Co.Un.)		70,001
Cadbury (Lib.)	65,200 + 14,000	= 79,200
Berkeley (Co.Lib.)	51,000 + 5000	= 56,000
Jones (Lab.)	45,100 + 500	= 45,600
Chamberlain (Co.Un.)	28,599 + 600	= 29,199
		280,000

Cadbury has now more than the quota, so we distribute his surplus votes as we did for Cholmondeley, with the following result:

Fourth Count

Cholmondeley (Co.Un.)		70,001
Cadbury (Lib.)		70,001
Berkeley (Co.Lib.)	56,000 + 4000	= 60,000
Jones (Lab.)	45,600 + 5000	= 50,600
Chamberlain (Co.Un.)	29,199 + 199	= 29,398
		280,000

[1] For simplicity of exposition, it is assumed that each voter makes a full list of preferences. Actually, many would prefer simply to vote for one member, or for Coalition members or Liberal members only.

This time, Chamberlain must go, so we divide his votes according to their next preferences, and reach this conclusion:

Fifth Count

Cholmondeley (Co.Un.)		70,001
Cadbury (Lib.)		70,001
Berkeley (Co.Lib.)	60,000 + 29,000 =	89,000
Jones (Lab.)	50,600 + 398 =	50,998
		280,000

The final result is, then, that this constituency, which would have been represented by three Coalition members if it had been divided up, is represented by two Coalition supporters and a member of the Liberal Opposition. Moreover, a slight increase in the popularity of the Labour party would have given Jones a quota and would have secured his election instead of Berkeley.

This system was recommended by the Speaker's Conference, but it was rejected by the House of Commons. It was restored by the House of Lords, which however rejected the alternative vote. Eventually the two Houses reached a compromise under which both the alternative vote and the single transferable vote disappeared, except that the single transferable vote was retained for the university constituencies returning two or more members. There was also a provision by which commissioners were to prepare a scheme for the election of one hundred members on the principle of proportional representation. No action was ever taken on it, and it was repealed in 1927 as obsolete.

The alternative vote and proportional representation are at first sight so attractive that the case for them appears to be unanswerable. It may be noted that if proportional representation is good for the towns, or for one hundred constituencies, it is good for the whole country, and in that case there is no need for the alternative vote, which is admitted to be a device less satisfactory than proportional representation. There is, however, this qualification, that towns are compact constituencies, whereas some rural constituencies cover large areas. For proportional representation to work effectively there ought to be at least three members to a constituency, so that, for instance, the three vast constituencies in the North of Scotland would form a single constituency covering perhaps four million acres.

Let us first consider the alternative vote. Its first result would be to encourage three-cornered or four-cornered contests, because a candidate who could not hope to win on a majority or a plurality[1] would hope to win on second preferences. To come down to practical politics, it would have encouraged the Labour party to put up more candidates before 1914, because Labour candidates would expect to receive the second preferences of Liberal voters; and it would have encouraged the Liberal party to put up more candidates since 1918, because Liberal candidates would expect to get the second preferences of both Conservatives and Labour voters. In the second place, and as a consequence, the occasions on which the Government had not a majority in the House of Commons would be more frequent. It is possible that no party would have had a majority in 1922, 1923, 1924, 1929, 1950, 1951 and 1964—though of course there would have been more elections, because minority Governments dissolve more readily than majority Governments.

In the third place, it would demand bargains between the parties before an election and, if it resulted in no party having a majority, bargains in the House or else Coalition Governments. There would be, too, bargains between individual candidates and a process of angling for second preferences by means of election pledges. This was described in 1918 as 'log-rolling'. In one of the debates in the House of Commons, Sir George Younger showed what would have been the result of the elections of 1910 if there had been compacts between the various parties, and the electors had obeyed party requests as to the distribution of their second

---

[1] This convenient American term is used to cover the case of a candidate who is elected because he has most votes, but not an absolute majority of the votes.

preferences. It is more interesting to take the election of 1929, where more than half the members secured election on a plurality. The result may be tabulated as follows:[1]

	Cons.	Lib.	Lab.	Others	Government
Actual result	260	59	287	9	Labour (minority)
Cons.-Lib. 'deal'	368	76	162	9	Conservative
Cons.-Lab. 'deal'	291	19	276	9	Conservative (minority) or Coalition
Lab.-Lib. 'deal'	112	139	354	9	Labour

This is far too simplified to be accurate: many electors would refuse to follow the party decision; and the working would be complicated by local 'deals'. The table does show, however, that elections might be determined not so much by the electors as by the party managers.

In the fourth place, the alternative vote system equates the second preferences, given by those who voted for the candidates with fewest first preferences, with the first preferences given to the others. Clearly, a first preference is more important than a second preference. The result is to secure the election not of the candidate who is approved by the largest group, but of *one* of the candidates who is not seriously objected to. This is shown by dividing out the second preferences in the case of each candidate in turn.[2]

[1] Where the 'deal' would not have applied, the actual result is taken.
[2] Thus

   (1) First preferences only:

Cholmondeley (Cons.)	20,000
Cadbury (Lib.)	15,000
Jones (Lab.)	10,000

   (2) Divide Jones's second preferences:

Cadbury (Lib.)	23,000
Cholmondeley (Cons.)	22,000

   (3) Divide Cadbury's second preferences:

Cholmondeley (Cons.)	29,000
Jones (Lab.)	16,000

   (4) Divide Cholmondeley's second preferences:

Cadbury (Lib.)	33,000
Jones (Lab.)	12,000

The only certain result is that the electors do not want Jones Under the alternative vote system Cadbury is elected, but only one-third of the electorate really wants him to be elected. In actual practice, of course, the result would be determined by 'log-rolling'.

25

In one of the House of Commons debates, Sir F. E. Smith (afterwards the first Lord Birkenhead) said that the previous speaker had given sixteen reasons against proportional representation. Some of the reasons usually stated against it can be dismissed in a few words. It clearly requires multiple constituencies, and thus would sometimes necessitate constituencies large in area. On the whole, however, the United Kingdom is densely populated, and multiple constituencies even in the north of Scotland would be small compared with some of the single-member constituencies in Canada, Australia, Asia or Africa. Again, it is argued that the contact between members and constituents would be less close—undoubtedly it would be, but this is not very important, partly because the elector really votes for a party, and partly because, in many cases, he would be able to communicate with a member with whose politics he sympathised. The Liberal members really charge themselves with the complaints of all Liberals in the country, and some electors write to members belonging to other constituencies, simply because they would rather write to the devil than to their own member. Another objection is that proportional representation is too complicated—but it is complicated for the returning officer, not for the voter, who merely has to write numbers against the candidates' names; and, the whole electorate being literate, the number of spoilt papers would be few. Finally, proportional representation cannot be applied to by-elections; but that is no reason for not applying it to general elections.

Proportional representation has, however, one consequence, which can be regarded as good or bad according to one's point of view. Our present system helps to maintain the two-party system; and when that system breaks up, as during the growth of the Labour party, it is a strong force towards compelling its return. Whether this is desirable or not depends on whether the two-party system is good or bad. Reasons are given in the next chapter for suggesting that it is good; but many disagree, particularly those who belong to middle parties which are being crushed out. It is significant that, while the Liberal party has favoured proportional representation consistently since 1918, neither the Conservative party nor the Labour party has given any support—though opinion was very divided in 1917–18, when party lines were fluid.

In order to be elected under the present system, a candidate must secure the highest number of votes. If he starts with a party 'label' he is certain of the party votes. The average elector has made up his mind to vote for one party or another. What he is doing in fact is to choose that party which he wishes to see forming a Government. Since 1945 he has had to choose between the Conservative party and the Labour party. No other party has had enough candidates to secure a majority and, except in 1964, at least 90 per cent of the votes have been given to those two parties. The elector has one vote, and he naturally wishes to use it to support the existing Government or to put another in its place. This is partly the cause, but mainly the consequence, of the two-party system. Because the elector wants to help choose a Government, therefore he votes for the Government or the chief Opposition party. But he wants to help choose a Government because we have the two-party system and because he has only one vote.

If his vote is transferable, however, other motives come into operation. He not only wants to bring one party *in*; he also wants to keep one party *out*. Thus, most Conservatives would prefer a Liberal to a Labour member: and most Labour voters would prefer a Liberal to a Conservative. Accordingly, three-corner fights would operate to the benefit of the Liberal party. The result might be—it probably would have been at any election since 1918 except those of 1931 and 1945—that no party would have a majority. Moreover, this would not be a temporary phase, as we thought it between 1922 and 1935, but a permanent feature. Once this had happened, and we had departed from the two-party system,

27

the electors would no longer vote for a Government but for a group. The main buttress of the two-party system would be destroyed, and not only would later preferences be distributed, but so would first preferences. Further, the groups would not be limited to the Conservative, Liberal and Labour parties. Any section of opinion which could secure enough preferences in any constituency—and electors would vote according to their special interests and not according to their view as to what Government should be in power—would put up a candidate. Proportional representation has therefore been described as a movement for the encouragement of 'sects'. Our present system induces sectional opinions to find representation within a party, or to secure their acceptance by members of both parties. Under proportional representation they would be the basis of separate parties.

We should thus have a House of Commons divided not into Government and Opposition but into *blocs*. Every Government would be a coalition. Moreover, it would not be the kind of coalition which we had in 1918–22 or 1931–39. The parties in those coalitions had separate organisations, but they fought elections as units. The Government candidatures were divided up by agreement among the parties. A Coalition Liberal did not oppose a Coalition Unionist; nor did a Liberal National oppose a Conservative. Under proportional representation we should have much less stable coalitions, without electoral pacts, except on a temporary basis. The elector would vote for candidates or parties not, as he does now, for a Government.

CHAPTER II

GOVERNMENT BY PARTY

I. THE POLITY OF PARTIES

John Stuart Mill wrote a book on *Representative Government* without mentioning parties. A realistic survey of the British Constitution to-day must begin and end with parties and discuss them at length in the middle. There are some who deplore the influence of parties. They assert that the tasks of government are too urgent and complicated to be the subject of partisan controversy. They would wish Parliament to be a 'Council of State' to consider, free from party bias, the nature of the problems that beset the community and the solutions that might be devised to meet them. They want to pool the intelligence of the nation, not to divide it into two parts by the parliamentary gangway. They dislike debate when action is what is required. They urge statesmen to 'pull together', and not to have bow side cry 'forward', while stroke side cries 'back'.

It is an attractive picture. The difficulty, to continue the rowing metaphor, is that there is no agreement as to who shall be cox. One cannot expect either side to pull with a will if cox announces his intention of steering the boat over the weir: and the difficulty in politics is that there are different views as to where the weirs are to be found. The assumption upon which democracy is based is that inevitably there are differing views as to the policy which a Government should follow. No honest man is entitled to assume that one policy is better than another; all that he can say is that he thinks that one is better. It will generally be found that the critic who asserts that parties are unnecessary has a belief in the rightness of his own opinion so profound that he does not realise

29

that it is a partisan opinion. He wants a 'Council of State' to carry out his policy. The true democrat has a suspicion that he may not always be right. He is therefore tolerant of other people's opinions. Moreover, since there is no court of appeal by which a controversy can be determined, he acquiesces in the system of counting votes. A majority may not be best capable of determining what is good for humanity, but it is probably better able than the minority to determine what is good for the majority; if the majority is also tolerant and sensible, it will not in the process injure the minority more than it can help.

Tolerance in this country is a principle of long standing. It has developed gradually from the struggles of the seventeenth century. It has been carried out in the laws; but it is still more an attitude of mind. It is, however, not tolerance alone that makes democratic government work. With us, the majority is not permanent. It is based upon differing views of personal and national interest, views which are susceptible of change and, in a sufficient number of persons, do change from time to time. Not only do opinions fluctuate, but they fluctuate sometimes violently, and the 'swing of the pendulum' is a familiar feature of British politics. Consequently, parties can and do appeal to reason. Majorities are unstable, and the Opposition of to-day is the Government of tomorrow. This important fact must not be forgotten, for it enables the minority to submit peacefully and even cheerfully to the fulfilment of the policy of the majority. It would be quite different if the minority were always a minority, if it were liable to oppression by the majority, and if in no circumstances could its views prevail.

Political parties founded on factors which are not matters of opinion are a danger. I can be Conservative to-day and Socialist tomorrow. Both parties angle for my support, and therefore are careful of my interests. Apart from the fact that toleration extends to Jews as to Gentiles, a Government will not oppress Jews so long as Jewish voters support both parties. Similarly, there will be no 'injustice to Scotland' so long as Scots vote Conservative, Liberal and Labour and not Scottish Nationalist. If, however, Englishmen vote for an English party and Scots for a Scottish party, either Scotland will be oppressed or the Union will be destroyed. To say this is not necessarily to blame the Irish; the Irish movement arose while there was discrimination on the ground of religion; and it does not necessarily follow that the Union ought to have been preserved either in respect of Ireland or in respect of Scotland. All that is implied in the present argument is that the party system will not work unless it is based on factors of opinion which can change. A Conservative Government might persuade me to become a Conservative overnight. It cannot change my ancestry, my language, my tribe or caste (if I had one), my religion, or even my economic status.

Nor does it follow that these factors are not important in the choice of party. We shall see that some of them have had profound influence on the development and bias of the British parties: but no party capable of forming a Government has been founded essentially on any unchangeable factor or on any combination of such factors. British parties are catholic in the true sense. Neither in their organisation nor in the implications of their policy have they excluded any person from supporting them, on grounds of ancestry, religion or even economic status. The Conservative party is not all capitalists, nor is the Labour party made up entirely of workers.

This catholicity has enabled the parties to be wide in the scope of their policies. Each party contains members and attracts supporters of differing opinions. It has enabled us to differentiate between opposition and obstruction. The Irish Nationalist party obstructed because it insisted on its own programme. Other parties oppose because they want to appeal to the people to support their own programme. Only occasionally—as with the Parliament Bill of 1911 and the Trade Disputes and Trade Unions Bill of 1927—does a

British party obstruct; and it does so then because the party in opposition believes that the Government is taking an unfair advantage of its temporary majority. It is not true, therefore, that the parties are pulling in different directions. Only one party is pulling, and the other is merely criticising. The Opposition warns; and in warning it seeks to change opinion. It says that certain consequences will follow; if these consequences do follow, and they appear undesirable to a few hundred thousand electors, the Government will be overthrown and policy will be diverted along different lines.

Moreover this same catholicity, this fact that Government and Opposition appeal to a few hundred thousand electors, produces the consequence that the actual division of opinion is not very precise. There are fundamentally opposed views in the House of Commons, but they are generally not majority opinions on either side. Bagehot long ago pointed out that the differences between Liberals and Conservatives were not great. It is true that he was writing only twenty years after Peel had adopted Cobden's policy by repealing the Corn Laws, and only a year or so after Palmerston governed the country with the tacit consent of the Conservative party. There have been issues which have fiercely divided the country, like Home Rule in 1886 and the Parliament Bill in 1910. Yet a Conservative majority gave Home Rule and much more to Ireland, and Bonar Law sat at Asquith's right hand before the Parliament of 1910 expired. Nor has the rise of the Labour party and the demand for socialism made much difference. We are all collectivists and have been for half-a-century. On this subject more must be said; but it is part of the explanation of the fact that the British party system does not prevent government. It makes it more consonant with public opinion.

No doubt parliamentary opposition slows up the governmental machine. It would be easier to carry out a policy if it were not subject to criticism. The time between decision and the first stage of execution is longer than in a dictatorship, except when rapid execution is really urgent—and then the British machine is the most rapid in the world, for quite different reasons. It is often said that a democracy necessarily works more slowly than a dictatorship. It must be remembered, however, that the process between the discovery of the initial fault or complaint and the remedying of that fault is necessarily a complicated one. It has come up through the official strata until it reaches the point at which a decision can be taken. There follows the period of decision (which may be longer with a single dictator than with a Cabinet). Then comes the issue of the necessary orders; and finally there is another process of percolation through the official strata until the remedy is applied. The process is much the same in all countries. If there is a legislature, however, it sometimes happens that no orders can be issued until legislation has been passed; and here the party system may interpose delay. The other parts of the procedure may, however, be shorter; and generally they are shorter in Great Britain than they were in Germany under Hitler, for example. Moreover, the parliamentary system has the great advantage that a particular fault may be brought to the top stratum by a question or a debate in Parliament. The German citizen could reach Hitler only through an immense bureaucracy. Any British subject can reach the Cabinet at once through his member. Further, the policy decided upon depends in all countries upon the currents of public opinion. In a dictatorship it is most difficult to ascertain them, particularly if the press is muzzled. In Great Britain opinion is vocal, and primarily in Parliament. The Cabinet, so to speak, goes to Parliament every afternoon and asks if there are any complaints; and at once from the Opposition there arises a chorus of 'Yes, Sir'.

Nevertheless, much party controversy is shadow boxing or (as a Conservative member who was too intelligent for his constituency put it) the fighting of sham battles with wooden swords. The Government consists of and is supported by politicians who want to win the next election. Accordingly,

33

it must never make a mistake, or at least admit it. On the other hand, the Opposition consists of politicians who want to achieve office at the next election. It therefore picks on those actions of the Government which it believes to be most open to criticism. Both sides exaggerate, not as much in the House of Commons as on public platforms outside, but enough to give the reader of popular newspapers the impression that the House of Commons is as noisy and as inconclusive as a dog-fight. On the whole common sense, which is available on both sides of the House, manages to prevail; but sometimes, after two 'good fighting speeches', one on each side of the House, one wonders if truth, which probably lies somewhere in the middle, would not prevail more easily if nobody made 'fighting speeches'. This is, however, a recent perversion of the party conflict, due primarily to the invention of the halfpenny newspaper. It seems to be on its way out because on television tub-thumping is the comedian's speciality, while politicians have to be very reasonable gentlemen, politely differing as to which of them has slightly more reason than the other.

2. A SHORT HISTORY OF THE PARTIES

British parties, like the British Constitution itself, have a long history. How long it is depends upon what aspect of party the historian has in mind. The parties are now complex organisations, made up of different institutions with different functions, and each institution and each function has its own history. Like all political institutions, political parties evolve under the influence of different people and to meet changing circumstances. Not all the characteristics of the major parties existed fifty years ago; but others of those characteristics existed three hundred years ago. Indeed, if one speaks of 'conservatism' and 'liberalism' with small letters, it is clear that ideas or attitudes of this kind have existed since men first became political animals. Even the Labour party, whose existence as an organisation can be traced back no further than 1899 (though some of its constituent members are older), has been provided by its historians with a long history. It was, in its origin, an organisation to forward the interests of the working class through political action; and accordingly its historians go back to the Peasants' Revolt of 1381.

It is, however, safer to begin in 1642, when the politically-conscious section of the population—a small segment—divided into royalists and Parliament men. It was not a case of the conservatives fighting for King Charles I and the reformers for Parliament; the division was complicated enough for the individual and even more complicated for the family, which in many cases was split by the civil war. On the royalist side, however, there was an association of Church and King. The Long Parliament had been virtually unanimous in curbing the King's prerogative. It divided over his religious policy. Those who supported King Charles had virtually to support his view of religion; those who opposed his view of religion had to oppose King Charles. On the other hand, a slogan cannot control history: after 1645 the presbyterians were the royalists because the King had been defeated, and the problem was to know what to do with him. As in all revolutions, the dominant opinion moved to the left. When it had gone so far left that it could go no further it simply collapsed, and King Charles II came back from across the water in 1660 with almost unanimous support.

To say that the Puritans and the republicans went underground would be to give the impression of a subterranean resistance movement, which did not in fact exist. There were Puritans—a later generation called them dissenters—and there were republicans; but they were not politically organised. Vocal opinion was Anglican and royalist, but when it was suspected that Charles II had turned Roman Catholic and known that his brother and heir, James, Duke of York, had done so, those who were both royalists and Anglicans

35

had to decide whether they were so royalist that they had to accept a Roman Catholic king or so Anglican that they could not. It is significant that the first man to raise the issue publicly by means of the Bill to exclude the Duke of York from the throne, the first Earl of Shaftesbury (sometimes known as the first Whig), had had a presbyterian upbringing. Had James II not been so obstinately a Stuart there might have been a second civil war, with the issue complicated by a Roman Catholic king. In fact, however, opinion was once more virtually unanimous in 1688, as it had been in 1640. It divided again because some could not support the substitution of King William for King James, but wanted a regency or some other device which would not deny that James was at once king and unfit to rule. The Revolution of 1688 was not, therefore, a Whig Revolution, but it was appropriated by the Whigs because so many of the old royalists, or Tories, found themselves unable to accept the Revolution Settlement. It became even worse for the Tories when both of James' Protestant daughters, Mary II and Anne, died without issue surviving, and two royalist lines—not to mention James' male issue—had to be excluded because they were Roman Catholic. Not until after the defeat of Charles Edward Stuart, King James' grandson, at Culloden in 1746, could it really be said that the issue between Stuart and Hanoverian, Tory and Whig, was dead.

Though we speak of the Whig party and the Tory party, it must be remembered that the word 'party' implied no political organisation. Indeed, the term 'party' is in large measure an invention of the historians. The term Whig can be used of a politician who wholeheartedly accepted the Revolution Settlement and the Hanoverian Succession. The term Tory can be used of those who had doubts, whether those doubts induced them to go into exile with King James and his court, or to go into the country and live quietly, refusing to take the oath of allegiance to a king who was only remotely a Stuart, or to remain in London and privately toast 'the King across the water' while paying lip-service to the Hanoverians as *de facto* kings. On the other hand, the two words, Whig and Tory, were less used by contemporaries than by historians of a later generation, who read the divisions of 1688–1714 in terms of the party history of the nineteenth century.

If, however, we use modern terms at all, we must say that for most of the eighteenth century, and certainly from 1714 to 1784, Great Britain had not a party system but a group system. Each prominent politician had a group of supporters, never precisely defined, and never very large, known generally as his 'connexion'. When he took office, his connexion expected places, pensions and honours. When he went out of office he might or might not call out his connexion; and if he did call them out he usually found that his connexion was not as large as he had expected. Nor did all the connexions added together make up even one-half of the House of Commons. Most of the remainder seldom attended, or attended only for a short time during 'the season'. Since the executive government was still in the king's hands, it was not proper to oppose. A particular measure could be rejected because the king had been badly advised; but to oppose Government measures generally was 'factious', disloyal, and almost seditious. Generally, therefore, those who could not support the king's measures stayed away; and those who could support his measures, but did not deign to take office under a Hanoverian king or with Whig politicians, came to London only occasionally. Indeed, though the term 'Tory' was still used in the early years of George III, it was almost synonymous with 'independent country gentleman'. The Whig connexions were composed of country gentlemen; but they were not independent because by reason of family ties, personal loyalty, or personal interest, or perhaps all three, they were members of 'connexions'.

This association between Toryism and the independent

country gentlemen was not entirely accidental. Viscount Bolingbroke, who failed as a party politician, made quite a success of his new job as political pamphleteer. Being entirely opposed to the Whigs' 'system', he sought to show that party government—if we may call it so—was inconsistent with the British Constitution. He wanted the king to choose Ministers irrespective of party support, to rule by 'measures not men'. Whether George III ever modelled himself upon Bolingbroke's idea of a patriot king has been disputed by historians; but certainly Bolingbroke influenced the man who must be regarded (whatever he called himself) as the greatest of the Tories, William Pitt, Earl of Chatham. Pitt's connexions were Whig and he was quite ineffectual, except as a parliamentary orator, until he allied himself with one of the Whig connexions. His claim to be the greatest of the Tories rests upon his imperialist policy. 'Imperialist', like so many political terms, has now become a term of abuse. Imperialism is, of course, merely the British version of emotional nationalism. In Pitt's day the danger to British nationalism arose from the enormous power of the Bourbon kings of France. Pitt's contemporaries, supported by King George II, who was Elector of Hanover as well as King of Great Britain, sought to diminish that power by subsidising the German States. Pitt used this method, too; but his principal aim was to reduce French power at its extremities, in North America, the West Indies, Africa and India. Moreover he sought the support of the American colonists by treating them not as subordinates but as collaborators, Englishmen overseas, entitled to all the privileges and all the consideration of British subjects. His attitude implied that when the Governments of George III tried to coerce the American colonies, the Earl of Chatham was, with Edmund Burke, their greatest advocate in Parliament.

The party division did not become clear, however, until the French Revolution turned to political assassination and dictatorship. Most of the Tories had regarded the initial

Revolution as objectionable, in that it deprived the French king and the French aristocracy of their rights. Most of the Whigs welcomed it as a belated decision by the French to adopt the principles of the English Revolution of 1688. The effective leader of the Whigs, Charles James Fox, never wavered in his support for the principles of the French Revolution because he thought of it as a movement for the overthrow of tyrannical privilege. He was not a democrat but a good Whig, disliking absolute power whether in France or in Britain, disliking, too, the privileges of the aristocracy but respecting the rights of property and the principle of toleration. Throughout the French wars there was always a small Whig—and, indeed, we may almost say Liberal—Opposition. On the other hand, the main body of the Whigs, sometimes called 'the Old Corps', joined with the Tories, now led by Chatham's son, William Pitt the younger, in opposition to the French Revolution. With the Old Corps went their greatest propagandist, Edmund Burke. His speeches and essays laid the foundations of Conservatism for a century; for they justified the characteristics of the British Constitution in historical terms. It was the product of centuries of experience, not a rationalistic and Godless creation. Burke had been a severe critic of the Constitution as the 'man of business' of one of the Whig connexions; in the emotional atmosphere produced by the Terror he was prepared to defend every British institution because it had been produced by history.

From 1783, when the younger Pitt took office and especially from 1794, when the Old Corps finally went over, there was a gradual hardening of party lines. That is to say, there were fewer independents and it became easier to decide who was for the Government and who was against it, though even the most experienced commentators put a great many 'doubt-fuls' into their lists. 'Whipping in', or sending letters inviting 'our men' to attend and vote, had been practised intermittently since 1660 and did not become a regular practice until the nineteenth century. It became more common, on important debates, during the early years of that century. More attention, too, was paid to electioneering. This did not mean that there was anything like a 'Whig association' or 'Tory association' in every, or indeed in any, constituency. The first organisation of that kind was established in 1806 by Francis Place, the Radical tailor of Charing Cross, for the city of Westminster, though it did not become permanent. The first of the constituency associations still in existence was, it is believed, the Rochdale Reform Association, which was established in 1832. It was, indeed, after 1832 that most of the local party organisations were established.

Electioneering before 1832 depended upon the nature of the constituency. A few boroughs, the so-called 'rotten' or 'nomination' boroughs, were the property of wealthy individuals. One such was the Pitts' borough of Old Sarum, bought by the Earl of Chatham's grandfather. In such a borough the nominations were in effect vested in the owner. There were, too, many 'corporation boroughs',[1] though in many places one or both of the seats had come under the 'influence' of neighbouring landowners. Since most counties and many boroughs were under 'influence', and examples continued until 1884, it is necessary to explain what our forefathers meant by it.

In the main, 'influence' depended on the acceptance by everybody of the social hierarchy, especially in the rural areas and the small country towns. Examples can be seen in most parts of the democratic world to-day, though there are none in England. In the village or small town the squire and the parson (who was usually presented by the squire) were the important people, entitled to deference by long tradition. To 'vote against the estate', i.e. to vote against the candidates supported by the squire, was as disloyal as it is to-day to be a 'blackleg' in a trade dispute or to cheer for the wrong football team. The squire himself, however, was under social

1 I.e. those in which the choice was made by the mayor, aldermen and councillors.

obligations to a greater landowner, perhaps the great Earl of Loamshire himself. If the Earl's social hegemony throughout the county was undisputed, he could in effect nominate both county members and perhaps several borough members. On the other hand, there were few counties where this was so. If the Earl of Loamshire and Lord Blanktown both had influence, perhaps in different parts of the county, they might nominate rival candidates. Since the expense of an election might be enormous, however, they would probably be sensible and divide the seats. If there was a contest they would expect their 'friends' to help. The noble earl would call on the squire and express the hope that he bring his tenants and dependants to the poll. The squire would be delighted at my lord's condescension, and he and the parson would take pride in bringing in the freeholders of his village, and perhaps the shopkeepers of the neighbouring town, all of whom would be delighted to show their loyalty to the estate. If by chance the squire had a conscience and refused to advise his tenants how to vote, they would be very upset, for they simply could not choose between rival candidates nominated by such great men.

Not all counties and boroughs were under 'influence'. In a few counties the country gentlemen prided themselves on being independent, and actually met together to decide what candidate they (and their tenants and followers) should support. There were some boroughs where the franchise was so wide that anybody could win, provided that he had enough money to spend on bribery, treating, whiteboys (for defending one's voters and abducting one's opponents), bands, banners, streamers, ribands, and all the other devices which Charles Dickens attributed to 'Eatanswill' (probably the corrupt borough of Sudbury) and which were later listed in the Corrupt and Illegal Practices Prevention Act of 1883. There were even boroughs like Westminster or Preston with a franchise so wide that 'mob oratory' had to be employed, together with snob appeal (Fox had the advantage of having the beautiful Duchess of Devonshire on his side at West-minster), and the not very mysterious election device known to the contemporary reference books as 'money'.

We seem completely to have lost the party system; and so we have, almost. When the Government wanted to win an election—and until 1830 the Government won every election —it had to get on its side as many as possible of the people with 'influence'. The Earl of Loamshire was safe, for he was a convinced Tory; anyhow he was anxious to become a Marquis and he had several sons who were looking for pre-ferment in the Church, the Law, the Army and the Civil Service. My lord Blanktown, on the other hand, was a Whig. Could he be persuaded to withdraw his candidates by an offer of an earldom? If not, can we help the Earl of Loam-shire by a little money, or perhaps by ordering the excise officers to vote for his candidates, or otherwise by using the royal influence? The Earl, too, had his sanctions. If his candidates won, and the squire of Blackacre had voted against them, there would be no invitation to dinner for the lady of the manor; the Countess would publicly cut them at the hunt ball; there would be no Government jobs for the Blackacre sons. The squire, too, had his sanctions. He could not eject his freeholders, but he could eject his tenants at will; and freeholders often held leasehold property. A boot-maker or carpenter or tailor would expect no orders from the 'big house' if he voted against the estate.

William Cobbett called this system 'Old Corruption', and we must not minimise the corrupt elements in it. On the other hand, the corruption was exaggerated by the Reformers of 1830–32 because the Whigs had been out of office (except for a short break in 1805–6) since 1784. The exception always has more news value than the normal; and 'influence' was not usually corrupt. The fact that a thief will be sent to prison does not mean that men are honest because they do not want to be sent to prison. Loyalty to the estate was not due primarily to the fact that loyalty paid better than disloyalty.

We know that when public issues of great importance were under discussion, as in 1784 and 1830, public opinion did matter. A man like Wilberforce, who spent little, could win the great and expensive county of Yorkshire; and not all the money in the Mint could turn a Lowther out of Westmorland. The Greys spent vast sums in Northumberland, but only when the county was divided by the Reform Act could they win against a Percy.

The Reform Act was carried by a sweep of public opinion, but it did not seriously affect electoral arrangements. Since the new electors had to be registered, it was necessary to establish 'registration associations' in all large urban constituencies, and these were the origins of the local party associations. Moreover the political leaders in Parliament found it necessary to have more or less permanent central offices in London to encourage local associations, to find candidates for constituencies and constituencies for candidates, to collect and distribute funds, and so forth. The Conservative Central Office was not established until 1863 and the Liberal Central Association was formed in 1865. Meanwhile, however, the Conservatives had used the Carlton Club and the Liberals the Reform Club. We have, it will be noted, changed from Tories to Conservatives, and from Whigs to Liberals. The name 'Conservative' was adopted in 1832, apparently by way of a consensus of opinion, to indicate that the British Constitution was in danger from the Reformers and had to be conserved or protected. The Reform Act had been carried by Whigs, Canningite Tories (who had resigned in 1828–29 from the Duke of Wellington's Tory Ministry), and Radicals, all of whom called themselves Reformers. As that name became less popular, 'Liberal' began to take its place. After 1846, for instance, the Peelite Conservatives, who had supported the repeal of the Corn Laws, called themselves 'liberal conservatives' i.e. Conservatives who, unlike the 'country party', supported a liberal economic policy. Palmerston was the last of the Canningites;

and after his death in 1865 most supporters of Gladstone (a 'liberal conservative') called themselves Liberals. What is more, by the period of the great contest between Gladstone and Disraeli, nearly every member of Parliament was either a Liberal or a Conservative.

In 1867 Disraeli 'dished the Whigs' by introducing household franchise in the towns, thus increasing the electorate from some 5 per cent. of the population to 16 per cent. He had hoped that the workers of the towns would vote Conservative, and many of them did, though not enough to give him a majority. He therefore undertook a reorganisation—or strictly speaking a development—of party organisations in the constituencies. He did not entirely succeed, for two reasons. First, the idea of working-men joining in clubs and associations with the comparatively wealthy was not everywhere accepted; and, though Disraeli did not like them much, Conservative Working-Men's Associations continued as separate organisations in many towns, especially in Conservative Lancashire. Secondly, the big landowners had not yet realised that winning elections by 'influence' was becoming more difficult, even in the counties, and accordingly there was considerable resistance to the idea of squire, parson and tenant sitting on the same committee.

Nevertheless, Disraeli won the election of 1874, and it was now for the Liberals to look to their organisation. Gladstone was not good at this kind of thing, though he was very good at the 'mob oratory' which swayed urban electorates. Moreover he resigned his leadership to the Marquis of Hartington, a Whig of the old school (his family, the Cavendishes, had been one of the great Whig families). The lead was therefore taken by young Joseph Chamberlain, who organised his own city of Birmingham on the 'Birmingham plan'—actually invented by William Harris, another Birmingham Radical, but enthusiastically developed by Chamberlain after the defeat of 1874. The 'Birmingham plan', usually known as 'Joe's Caucus', was an ingenious arrangement based upon ward committees, which nevertheless enabled the middle-class leaders to dominate the association. It was a permanent arrangement, under which the association conducted regular propaganda between elections and fought local as well as national elections. In effect all the local parties of modern times are based upon 'Joe's Caucus', though in 1880 only the large towns had followed the Birmingham plan.

One of the changes of 1868, not invented by Disraeli but blessed by him, was the establishment of a federation of Conservative associations under the name of the National Union of Conservative and Constitutional Associations. It was not an important body, and when after the defeat of 1880 Lord Randolph Churchill tried to take power out of the hands of the Conservative Central Office and vest it in the National Union he was defeated. Meanwhile, however, Chamberlain had founded the National Liberal Federation as a Radical organisation. When Chamberlain seceded over Home Rule in 1886 the Federation stood by Gladstone. It therefore assumed to itself the responsibility of formulating a programme in a series of resolutions, which collectively became known as the Newcastle Programme. Though not binding on the Liberal leaders, it was a considerable embarrassment to them after the general election of 1892.

Having dealt at some length with party organisation, we have at last reverted to party policy. In 1832 'Reform' seemed to be triumphant; and the reform of the electorate was followed by the reform of the poor law and the reform of municipal corporations. By 1837, however, a reaction had set in. The Reformed Constitution was really not very different from 'Old Corruption'. There had been a gradual improvement in the central machinery under the younger Pitt and his successors; but in most constituencies after 1832, as before, there was a mixture of corruption and 'influence'. Sir Robert Peel, who led the Conservative party after 1834, persuaded his supporters to accept the Reform Act and to work the Reformed Constitution. In 1841 the Conservatives

won a majority and Peel at once took office. He was a manu-
facturer's son who sympathised with the manufacturing
interest and had collaborated with Huskisson in freeing trade
after 1824. The great body of his supporters, however, were
the 'country party', the landed gentry who disliked the new
factory system and insisted that the British Constitution was
founded upon land. The battle was fought over the repeal
of the Corn Laws in 1846. A body of northern manufacturers
and merchants, led by Cobden and Bright, had since 1838
been conducting a fierce (and not very scrupulous) agitation
for the repeal of the Corn Laws, which protected agriculture
and therefore kept up the price of bread and the wages of
factory workers. The great potato famine in Ireland in
1845–46 forced Peel to act; and, when he found that the
Whigs would not do the job for him (though they were
anxious to profit from his difficulties) he proposed and
carried the repeal of the Corn Laws with Whig support.
Inevitably the Conservative party split, the landed interest
being led by Disraeli under the more or less nominal leadership of Lord George Bentinck.

British politics thus obtained a class basis. On the one side
was the landed interest, who at first called themselves 'Protectionists' but eventually returned to the name 'Conservatives'. On the other side was a miscellaneous collection of
Whigs, Radicals and Peelites (or Liberal Conservatives),
bound together by the principles of free trade, and supported
by most of the manufacturing and mercantile interests.
These became, after the middle of the century, and definitely
after 1865, the Liberal party. This is, of course, a very
generalised interpretation. Industrial Lancashire, for instance, was mostly Conservative, while both industrial
Yorkshire and rural Wales (and much of the rural West of
England) were mostly Liberal. The Conservatives were
mostly Anglicans, while the dissenters and the Methodists
(who were strictly not dissenters) gradually coalesced in the
Nonconformist interest, which supported the Liberal party

except in 1874 (when it was annoyed with the Liberal Education Act of 1870). This, however, is another aspect of the class division, because the landed interest was almost exclusively Anglican, while the Nonconformists were strong among the manufacturing interest.

In fact, however, there was little between the parties from 1852 to 1865. The enfranchisement of the urban working-class in 1867 had no immediate effects, though in the longer run it showed itself in a conflict between employers and employees. Since most of the employers were at first Liberals, Disraeli calculated that the workers would vote Conservative; and many of them did. On the other hand, the old division between the landed interest and the manu-facturing interest became less important as the consequences of industrialisation spread. Landed proprietors were inter-ested in mines, railways and urban rents. After 1862 the development of the limited liability company enabled the landowners to buy shares without engaging in trade. More-over to make profits from land against foreign competition it was necessary to develop scientific farming. The social system of village and county, which enabled the landed interest to 'influence' elections, broke down when the squire became either an absentee landlord or a scientific farmer. The tenant was more concerned with rent and wages than with social obligations to the squire. The destruction of 'influence' was completed by the Reform Act of 1884, which enfranchised the agricultural workers and the workers of the small towns which were not boroughs.

The new class alignment became clearer in 1886, when most of the Whigs defected from Gladstone's Liberal party over Home Rule for Ireland. This seems to be an irrelevant issue, but its relevance was twofold. First, the Conservative party had become increasingly imperialist since 1852, and this imperialism strongly affected the Whigs. Secondly, the growing strength of the Radical Movement, led by Sir Charles Dilke and Joseph Chamberlain, had made it more and more difficult for the Whigs to support the Liberal party; indeed the Liberal Government of 1880 to 1885 had been so acutely divided that it had done very little. Because of the great social changes of the Victorian era, there was little difference between the Whigs and the Conservatives. Joseph Chamberlain, as well as the Whigs, defected in 1886, but (outside Birmingham and its neighbourhood) he carried little Radical support. In effect, the Conservative party and its allies the Liberal Unionists represented 'property' after 1886, while those who lived on salaries and wages tended to be Liberal.

The effect of the Liberal split in 1886 was, however, that the Conservatives dominated English politics (though in 1892 they lost the election because of Welsh, Scottish and Irish support for the Liberals and Home Rulers) from 1886 to 1905. This was the great period of Conservative imperialism, with the ex-Radical and ex-republican Joseph Chamberlain as the arch-imperialist. The 'khaki' election of 1900, so-called because what seemed to be the end of the war in South Africa was seized upon as an opportunity to use war hysteria to secure a Conservative victory, carried this imperialism into the twentieth century. It was then that imperialism became a naughty word, for it was alleged by the Liberal propagandists—not wholly fairly—that imperialism was a device to enable capitalists to increase their profits. Joseph Chamberlain, who never forgot that politicians had to win votes, tried to continue the imperialist tradition after the end of the South African war in 1902 by raising the standard of 'Tariff Reform', i.e. Protection (though that, too, was a naughty word) combined with Imperial preference or even Empire Free Trade. This unified the Liberals (who had been divided over the South African War) and split the Conservatives, with the result that the Liberal party won a large majority in 1906.

There was, however, a new phenomenon. Though the urban workers had obtained the vote in 1868 and the rural workers in 1885, the parties made little attempt to produce policies which would attract the new voters. Disraeli flirted with them, but really had nothing to offer; Chamberlain's *Radical Programme* of 1884 was a good first attempt at a working-class policy, but it disappeared when Chamberlain went Unionist in 1886; the Liberal's Newcastle Programme of 1891 offered something to the workers, as it offered something to everybody. Except in mining areas, however, working-class candidates could not get Liberal nominations. The trade unions had been developing since the early years of the century, but they were small 'craft unions' more concerned with their friendly society benefits than with militant trade-unionism or politics. The Trades Union Congress, founded in 1868, had been small and not very effective, though it did secure legislation in relief of trade unions in 1871 and 1875. There was, too, a small socialist movement, which resulted in the establishment of the Social Democratic Union (Marxist) in 1881 and the Fabian Society (Non-Marxist) in 1883. The Independent Labour party, established in 1893, consisted mainly of (non-Marxist) socialists, but had used the name 'Labour' in order to attract trade union support. In and around 1889 a 'new unionism' developed as a movement among the unskilled workers, which had considerable success in improving the conditions of the worst-paid section of the workers. Later in the 'nineties, however, the employers began 'counter-attacking', by using legal machinery to obstruct strikes, peaceful picketing, and trade-union militancy generally. This induced the Trades Union Congress to modify their attitude of aloofness from politics. A special conference of trade unions and socialist societies was summoned in 1899 to consider means for securing the return of Labour members to Parliament. Few thought of this development as likely to produce a Labour Government, even in the long run. The failure of the Liberals to adopt a specifically Labour policy; the unwillingness of Liberal associations to support working-class

49

candidates; the split in the Liberal party which resulted from Lloyd George's ousting of Asquith in 1916 and the use of a Coalition 'coupon' against the independent Liberals in 1918; and generally the enormous growth of trade unionism between 1900 and 1922; these factors led to the Labour party supplanting the Liberal party as the alternative Government. From 1922 most electors realised that, to have influence on policy, it was necessary to vote either Conservative or Labour.

The Labour party was peculiar in that it was organised outside Parliament: the Conservative and Liberal parties developed their organisations outside Parliament in order to support parties already existing in Parliament. Moreover, the Labour party was built on existing organisations, the trade unions and socialist societies. Though in 1918 it developed a constituency organisation, too—at the same time as it adopted a Fabian socialist programme—the party constitution was so devised as to give ultimate control to the trade unions, through the block vote, of the party conference, which is the policy-making body.

3. THE CHARACTER OF THE PARTIES

Though the Labour party is, historically, an extra-parliamentary party seeking representation in Parliament, while the Conservative party or the Liberal party is an intra-parliamentary party with a large extra-parliamentary organisation, the result is much the same. The essence of the party, and in organisational terms its objective, is the parliamentary party consisting of members of Parliament and peers. The peers have both the advantages and the disadvantages of not having constituents to keep them in order. The number of peers active in Parliament is small, even in the Conservative party, and for the most part they are life peers, or hereditary peers of the first generation who have been in the House of Commons. As such, they are usually orthodox party men who do not need to be kept in order; they toe the party line almost by instinct. Nevertheless, there is rather more cross-voting in the House of Lords than in the House of Commons. In the latter House it is thought necessary that the whips should be put on—i.e. that members should vote according to party—in respect of almost every motion, and that members should always obey the whip. The Labour party expressly and the other parties by implication allow a member with conscientious scruples—whatever that may mean—to abstain from voting on a particular issue. The whips are less fierce than they are commonly represented to be. Normally they are persuasive people of the 'old boy' type—the member is expected to support the party for the reasons that are used to persuade Smith minor to support the school. There is a sanction against a member who consistently disobeys the whip; but examples of its use are rare because the local party organisations are usually more orthodox than the whips and begin to ask questions of their member long before the withdrawal of the whip is contemplated. More often, members themselves sometimes refuse the whip, especially in the early stages of a Parliament—for most members become more orthodox as a general election approaches. A political peer is very like a politician in the other House; and so the fact that he has no constituents to keep him in order is usually irrelevant. Nevertheless, there are a few active peers who do not take a whip; and occasionally a peer who does take it nevertheless disobeys it. The occasions are few but significant; for the peers tend to show, more readily than the members of the House of Commons, when the Government's case is really not very convincing.

The purpose of the party in Parliament is to support the Government in carrying out the party policy; or, if the party is in Opposition, criticise the Government in so far as it fails to carry out the policy of the party in Opposition. Since a Government rarely maintains its majority for more than ten years, the Opposition party can assume that within such period, or less, it will be required to assume office. This fact places considerable limitations upon its power to oppose. As we shall see, a party depends for its electoral support more upon its general reputation than upon its current policies. What used to be the heckler's favourite question, 'What did Mr Gladstone say in 1868?', was not entirely irrelevant. Whatever Mr Gladstone said in 1868 was relevant for a whole generation. Hence a party in Opposition cannot afford to be irresponsible, to oppose for the sake of opposition, to obstruct the process of government, if it hopes to achieve power within ten or twenty years; for a bad reputation lives long. This does not mean that Oppositions are always states-manlike. Usually, in fact, there are 'ginger groups' on the back-benches whose members dislike the 'statesmanlike' attitude of the front-bench. Nevertheless, Government and Opposition alike have to follow consistent principles if they wish to appeal successfully to the electors over a long period. British parties cannot afford to be opportunist because, if they are, they lose their reputations for consistency, states-manship, and responsibility. Naturally, this does not apply to small parties like the Irish Nationalist party, or to the Communist party: it applies only where the party concerned hopes and expects to form a Government.

It follows that Government decisions and Opposition criticisms are related to consistent principles; and those principles, as we have seen, have a long history behind them. Their application to current controversies varies according to party. The Labour party, being primarily an extra-parliamentary party, has a complete organisation for working out what it usually calls 'policy statements'. Resolutions may come from the trade unions, socialist societies, con-stituency parties, or the National Executive Committee (N.E.C.) itself. They are generally so numerous that they have to be put into composite motions by the N.E.C. Policy statements as such, however, come from the N.E.C., which includes the party leader and other members of the parlia-mentary party. They are debated, often at length, by the

52

The swing of the pendulum: Government majorities since 1832

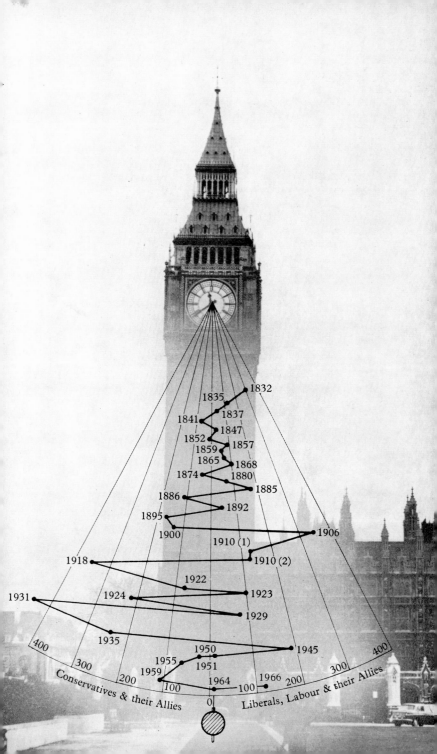

1832
1835
1837
1841
1847
1852
1857
1859
1865
1868
1874
1880
1885
1886
1892
1895
1900
1906
1910 (1)
1910 (2)
1918
1922
1923
1924
1929
1931
1935
1945
1950
1951
1955
1959
1964
1966

400
300
200
100
0
100
200
300
400

Conservatives & their Allies

Liberals, Labour & their Allies

annual conference of the Labour party, which thus exhibits to the electorate the range of differences within the party. In the other parties, the responsibility for policy rests with the leader: but he is aware of the currents of opinion in the National Union or the National Liberal Federation, as the case may be. The difference is, in fact, more formal than material. Formally, the annual conference binds the Labour party, whereas the National Union does not bind the Conservative party and the National Liberal Federation does not bind the Liberal party. If, however, the parties were to exchange organisations, the results would not be very different. The real difference is that Labour delegates, believing themselves to have—and, in a formal sense, having—the last word, exercise a more critical function than Conservative delegates, who know that the last word rests with the leader. The tradition of loyalty applies to both, though with greater force in the Conservative party, which for electoral reasons is more than usually effusive in its congratulations to the leadership when a strong minority thinks that the leader ought to be changed.

On the other hand, while the delegates to the Conservative and Liberal conferences represent only constituency organisations (which include special women's organisations, youth organisations, and trade union committees) the Labour party gives formal representation to affiliated trade unions, co-operative societies and socialist societies. Since voting goes by membership and not by the number of delegates, and some of the trade unions have hundreds of thousands of members, the trade unions can, by casting a block vote, dominate the Labour conference. This point, too, can be overemphasised. It often happens that the majority of trade union votes overrides the majority of constituency votes; but never are the trade unions on the one side and the constituencies on the other. On a real conflict of opinion both trade unions and constituencies will be divided.

Nor must it be thought that constituency associations, in

c

53

B.B.C. television's election scoreboard

any party, are truly representative of their respective electors. Most electors have nothing to do with politics save to vote at intervals. Only a minority subscribes to party funds. Of that minority only a minority attends party meetings; and of that minority of a minority only a minority is prepared to give time and trouble to party organisation. These party workers are, from the party point of view, the 'salt of the earth' because they spend so much time and energy on party affairs, without remuneration; but they are also a minority of a minority of a minority and therefore unrepresentative. The central party organisation, which has to be more concerned with votes than with the opinions of party workers, is often better informed of trends of opinion than are the local party organisations, which tend to mistake their own views for those of the electors.

In any event, a party organisation cannot effectively bind a Government, and therefore they cannot bind an Opposition when it becomes a Government. The term 'policy' is commonly used at different levels. There is, first, the historic policy of the Conservative party, which can be traced back to Disraeli, Burke, Chatham, Bolingbroke, and perhaps even Oliver Cromwell (who was not only a good 'imperialist' and a good 'protectionist', but also in several other ways a good conservative). There is, secondly, the policy which the Conservative party elaborated at the last election, a policy which was reasonably conservative, but was designed to catch the votes of those who were thought to be open to persuasion. There is, thirdly, the policy actually followed from week to week when the party is in office, or advocated from week to week when it is in Opposition. The policy followed by a Conservative Government is inspired by Conservative prejudices. The Government cannot forget—and is not allowed to forget—what the Conservative propagandists said at the last election; but what to do in a particular problem of foreign, Commonwealth, or home affairs must necessarily depend upon the circumstances in which that problem arises, on the views current among the electors at that time, and on the advice tendered not only by the party's own experts but by the civil service also. A party in Opposition cannot take advice from the civil service, though it often has a very good idea what that advice is; in all other respects the Opposition 'Shadow Cabinet' must exercise the same kind of day-to-day discretion as a Government.

In Opposition, this discretion can be limited by decisions at meetings of the whole parliamentary party, and by discussions with the party organisation outside. The Labour party makes full use of both, particularly because it is easy to call meetings of the N.E.C., or even joint meetings of the executives of the Labour party, the Trades Union Congress, and the Co-operative party. The Conservative party has no formal organisation, but the Conservative Private Members' Committee (the so-called 1922 Committee) and its warren of subject committees have much the same effect. No decisions are taken, but the sense of the meeting is usually obvious enough. When either party forms the Government, however, the system is modified. Unlike some of its progeny, the British Parliament has always distrusted the 'caucus', the party meeting which takes decisions binding on the Government. The method is used in local government, especially by the Labour party; but both in theory and in practice decisions in the central government are taken by the Cabinet on the basis of memoranda circulated by Ministers but drafted by civil servants. These memoranda cannot be circulated to other members of Parliament without serious risk of leakage of confidential information; private members cannot discuss matters informally with civil servants, as Cabinet Ministers can and do; moreover, all complicated Cabinet questions are referred to Cabinet committees, at which civil servants, officers of the defence forces, and so on, frequently are present. An appeal from the Cabinet to the 'caucus' ought therefore to be, and usually would be, an appeal from an informed body to an uninformed, or perhaps a misinformed, body. Governmental matters are too complicated to be decided by the light of pure reason (even if it be conceded, and usually it would not, that the 'caucus' had better reason than the Cabinet), or by the light of party prejudice: they ought to be founded on collective wisdom based on experience. Ministers have therefore always insisted on the reality of 'Ministerial responsibility', and have refused to share it with party committees or even with all-party committees. Party committees do meet; they are officially summoned in the sense that notices go out with the whips; but Ministers do not attend except by invitation and the discussions do not lead to conclusions binding upon Ministers individually or the Cabinet collectively.

Nevertheless, one of the essential tasks of a Government is to keep itself attuned to its electorate, for it wants to win the next election. To win the next election, it must secure the return of its supporters. It follows that the Government must retain the confidence of its supporters. Every Government takes decisions which many electors do not like; sometimes it has to take decisions which its supporters do not like. Supporters are not necessarily the best judges of an attractive policy, for they are in touch with the local associations in their constituencies; and these are often run, as we have seen, by a minority of a minority of a minority. Cabinet Ministers can judge of the effects of their decisions, not only from the views expressed by their supporters in the House, but also from the views expressed to the Conservative Central Office (or Labour Party Headquarters) by their paid agents in the regions and the constituencies, and from the newspapers, from sample polls taken by private initiative, and from their own long experience of the movements of opinion. Accordingly, the view taken by Cabinet Ministers of the way in which opinion is moving is seldom very wrong. All Governments become unpopular in the end: it is to that fact that we owe the changes of Government which we call the 'swing of the pendulum'; all Governments try to resist their inevitable unpopularity; and the result is a remarkably close correspondence between the actions of Government, viewed over a short term of years, and public opinion.

It is important to remember that parties are groups of politicians angling for popular support; but it is also important to remember that each has a historic mission. The Tories began as the supporters of a hereditary monarchy and became inevitably the party of order and stability, the party which stood by the British Constitution in the age of revolution. The Tories or Conservatives therefore represented the landed interest, the backbone of the country, and the system of government in Church and State founded upon it but challenged by the Reformers. The Whigs carried on, however feebly, the tradition of the civil war that, in the last resort, the representatives of the 'people' (in quotation marks because they were the people who mattered, not the 'mob' or common herd) must decide whether king and peers are properly exercising their powers. The Whigs therefore had no difficulties of conscience over the Revolution of 1688, or the Act of Settlement, or even a reasonable measure of tolerance for dissent. When a new liberalism developed after the French Revolution of 1789, it was to be found mainly among the Tories, but when the Tories split in 1829 the liberal or Canningite Tories were able to fuse with the Whigs upon a policy of constitutional reform. There was another Conservative split over the Corn Laws in 1846, which led after the middle of the century to the great controversy between the Conservatives and the Liberals under Disraeli and Gladstone.

Both were, in a sense, opportunist, and yet both had firm prejudices which made the Conservatives the 'imperialist' party and the Liberals the party of free trade, internationalism, and colonial constitutional development (or, in the current slogan, 'peace, retrenchment and reform'). This time the Liberals split, theoretically over Home Rule, or self-government for Ireland, but in fact over more fundamental issues. The Unionists were united by Home Rule: but they really represented the property owners, while the middle classes, especially the lower middle classes, were generally Liberal. The alliance of property and labour against the capitalists under Disraeli was merely temporary, because property and capital could not be distinguished. On the other hand, the alliance between the Liberal middle class and the working class also was temporary because the organised workers formed their own party.

These are generalisations. Ever since Disraeli 'dished the Whigs' in 1867 (and earlier in a few boroughs) many of the enfranchised workers have supported the Conservative party. Even in the trade unions there are workers who vote Conservative, though not many are politically active. There is evidence, too, that since 1918 a great many working-class women, especially those who 'don't hold with politics', have voted Conservative. On the other hand there are employers of labour among the active politicians of the Labour party and a fair leaven of Labour supporters among the salaried classes. The great strength of the Labour party from 1906 to 1951 (when its support in the electorate increased progressively, except in 1931) lay in the class-consciousness of organised labour, its sense of loyalty to 'people like us'. With the increase in the standard of living, the improvement both of the standard of education and of the educational ladder, and the diversification of employment (to all of which the propaganda of the Labour party contributed) that sense of class loyalty is, however, tending to disappear.

The Labour party was founded as the Labour Representative Council in 1899, by a few trade unions and socialist societies, for the sole purpose of securing the election to the House of Commons of working-class candidates who would, by political action, support the aims which the trade unions sought to achieve by industrial action, i.e. collective bargaining and, if necessary, strike action, to obtain better wages and conditions of labour. Even in industrial areas, however, they could not obtain seats except in alliance, avowed or tacit, with the Liberal party. By means of such alliances, the L.R.C. won 29 seats in 1906. The members so returned promptly called themselves the Labour party. On matters of broad policy they generally supported the Liberal Government, whose left wing, led by Lloyd George, realised that the essential task of the Liberal party was to retain the support of the industrial workers. The foundations of the Welfare State were therefore laid between 1906 and 1914—old age pensions, health insurance, unemployment insurance.

This effort was destroyed by the split in the Liberal party in 1916, when Lloyd George, in association with the Conservative leader, Bonar Law, ousted Asquith. Though efforts towards reconciliation were made after 1922, the split in the Liberal party had given the Labour party its opportunity. In 1918 the latter was reorganised on a constituency basis, i.e. local Labour parties were set up in an increasing number of constituencies with the intention of securing the election of Labour members both to the local councils and to Parliament. The close association with the trade unions was, however, retained. The local branches of the trade unions affiliated with the local Labour parties; the trade unions were given such representation at the annual conference of the Labour party that their block votes could, if it were necessary, decide all the issues of policy. At the same time a socialist, but non-Marxist, policy was adopted in principle, the nationalization of the means of production, distribution and exchange.

It is probable that the socialist policy never had the enthusiastic support of a majority of the electorate. Nevertheless, the Labour party had increasing support from the organised working-class, the great trade unions and their active members, especially in the lowlands of Scotland, the industrial north-east, the great coalfields, and the East End of London. It became clear in the 'thirties, however, that the division of opinion in the working-class, many of whose members continued to support the wealthier and generally more highly educated candidates of the Conservative party, was such that the Labour party could not get a majority without substantial support from the Radical opinion in the rapidly growing middle class.

The Labour party did get that support in the post-war reaction of 1945, a reaction against the Conservative domination from 1931 to 1940. The Labour leaders had joined the Churchill coalition in 1940 and had proved their capacity in the dark days of the war, for in the main they kept the home fires burning while Churchill concentrated on high strategy. The Labour Government of 1945, however, assumed responsibility for the inevitable post-war dislocation, and gained no credit for their projects of nationalization because the National Coal Board was as much a group of 'bosses' as the 'bosses' of the Mining Association before the war. The Government was defeated in 1951, and there were thirteen years of Conservative government.

The Conservatives benefited from increasing material prosperity, for which the Conservative Governments claimed credit. The manual workers more often than not earned more than the 'white collar' workers of the middle class, but they continued to vote for the working-class party so long as they continued to think of themselves as working-class, even when they owned their own houses, drove their own cars, and took their families for holidays in Mediterranean sunshine. This was so in the areas of heavy industries and the coalfields of the lowlands of Scotland, Yorkshire and South Wales. The areas of greatest prosperity were, however, the Midlands and the Home Counties around London. The Labour party could not win a majority unless it win a majority of seats in Greater London, where even the manual workers thought of themselves as 'middle class'.

This was the dilemma of the Labour party in the 'fifties and early 'sixties. In the older industrial areas, dominated by the concepts of the 'thirties, it had to appear as the party of the industrial workers, 'people like us': in the south-east it had to appear as the party of the new industrial revolution, the party which represented the technicians of the electronic age. Contrary to all precedent, the Labour vote went down in 1955 and 1959; but the strenuous efforts of the new men, many of them graduates of the University of Oxford, gave the Labour party a small majority in 1964. The dilemma remains, for the Labour party is still organised in close association with the trade unions; it still has a 'working-class image' while the working-class is disappearing; and it still proclaims, not very enthusiastically, the nationalization of the means of production, distribution and exchange. It has not yet been proved that the technicians want to turn their 'bosses' into quasi civil servants.

4. THE PARTY MACHINES

We have hitherto assumed that a party consists of a set of active politicians held together by personal loyalty or common political principles. Until the middle of the nineteenth century such an assumption would have been almost accurate. In the eighteenth century a statesman in embryo did not 'join a party', he merely looked round for a patron who owned or had 'influence' in a borough or a county and was willing to secure the election of 'a friend of Mr Pitt' or Mr Fox or Mr Canning. Even after the repeal of the Corn Laws in 1846 the Peelites were known as the friends or the followers of Sir Robert Peel. There is a relic still in the language of the House of Commons, where a member refers to another member of his own party as 'my honourable friend' instead of 'the honourable member'.

The party was, in fact, a group of members in the House of Commons, together with the peers of the same party or political persuasion; or perhaps it would be more accurate to say that it consisted of a group of Whig or Tory lords together with their sympathisers and dependents and nominees in the House of Commons. After 1832, however, it was no longer possible to secure a majority by the nomination and influence of landlords and close corporations, and it therefore became necessary in many constituencies to elaborate an organisation. Generally speaking, the initiative came from the constituencies or their members. Since the registration of electors depended primarily on private initiative, the essential function was to induce all supporters to claim registration and to watch that the other party did not secure the registration of unqualified persons. The responsibility for registration is now vested primarily in officials, and this function is therefore no longer of importance, but the size of the local electorate compels the maintenance of an elaborate organisation for securing a candidate, conducting propaganda at all times (and more intensively during an election), and, above all, organising the election campaign itself. This local organisation is largely autonomous; but the body now known as the National Union of Conservative and Unionist Associations was established, as we have seen, in 1868.

However, the Liberals captured most of the newly created working-class votes at the election of 1868. Accordingly, Disraeli decided that a more effective national organisation was required, and in 1870 he put the Conservative Central Office under his direct control, with a Party Manager appointed by him in immediate command. In 1872 it was arranged that the National Union should share offices with the Central Office, and that the two bodies should work in collaboration while retaining their separate organisations. Both conduct national propaganda, but the central funds are held by the Central Office and are thus under the control of the party leader.

The organisation of the Liberal party has sometimes led and sometimes followed that of the Conservative party. The Liberal Central Association, which compares with the Conservative Central Office, is however much more of a parliamentary secretariat, while the Liberal Party Organisation, which is based on the constituency parties, exercises many of the functions which in the Conservative party are exercised by the Central Office. In particular, it is the Organisation and not the Central Association which collects money for propaganda and assisting constituency associations. In other words, the funds of the Conservative party are under the direct control of the party leader; the funds of the Liberal party are under the control of the constituency associations.

The Labour party was founded by trade unions and socialist societies. It was only in 1918 that local Labour parties were formally established. Even now, the trade unions have larger representation in the National Executive Committee of the Labour party than the local Labour parties. There is, however, no leader and no 'Central Office'. The leader of the Parliamentary Labour party is elected by the members of Parliament every year, though he is usually re-elected. The chairman of the National Executive Committee changes from year to year. The statements of policy, which in the Conservative party are issued by the leader on his own responsibility, are in the Labour party approved after debate by the annual conference of the Labour party. The secretariat in Transport House is under the control of the National Executive Committee, which is elected every year by the conference.

This short account gives a very incomplete picture of the complexity of organisation. No reference has been made to women's sections and youth organisations, bodies like the Primrose League, the Fabian Society, the Bow Group, the societies of political agents, the educational activities of the Swinton Conservative College, the Liberal Summer School, and the National Council of Labour Colleges, and a score of other matters which would need to be examined in order to give a complete picture of political organisation. It is clear from what has been said, however, that it is not easy to found a party to compete with an established party. The central activities of a party in a normal year cost something like £100,000. A general election may cost a million pounds —in grants to candidates fighting 'forlorn hopes' and in propaganda. In addition each local association or party must find its own funds. In the Labour party these funds are obtained from small annual subscriptions and from grants by local branches of trade unions. The Conservative party can hope for more substantial contributions from its wealthier supporters, but since 1945 it has relied mainly, like the Labour party, on small annual subscriptions.

It is not, however, merely a question of money. It has been shown by experience that even when the money is available an election in a constituency can be lost by the absence of 'organisation'. This means all kinds of things, the week-to-week conduct of propaganda (and not merely during the three weeks before the election, but consistently), a thorough canvass, the organisation of public meetings, the provision of transport for lazy, sick and aged voters, the checking of persons who have voted in order to find out who can still be persuaded to vote, and generally a consistent 'drive' to urge the electors to the poll. It follows that few 'independents' can stand for election with any hope of success, and people who dislike the existing parties find great difficulty in establishing a new one to suit them. These conclusions are important for the discussion which follows.

5. THE TWO-PARTY SYSTEM

In 1882 W. S. Gilbert thought it comical

> How nature always does contrive
> That every boy and every gal
> That's born into this world alive
> Is either a little Liberal
> Or else a little Conservative.

He was, of course, using his poetic licence to ignore the Irish Nationalist party. Apart from them, there have always been smaller parties and groups—Radicals, Peelites, Liberal

Unionists, the Labour party, the Liberal party itself, Liberal Nationalists, National Labour members, the Co-operative party, the Independent Labour party, the Communist party, Common Wealth, the Scottish and Welsh Nationalist parties, etc. Since 1835 Governments without a party majority have been in office for twenty-eight years and Coalition Governments for thirty-four years. Yet in substance Gilbert was right; there is a 'natural' tendency for Great Britain to follow the two-party system. The Radicals merged into the Liberal party; the Peelites fused with the Whigs to form the Liberal party; the Liberal Unionists joined with the Conservative (and Unionist) party; the Labour party gradually displaced the Liberal party; and the National Liberals are not distinguishable from Conservatives.

English history since the seventeenth century gives the impression of a perpetual political duel: Royalists and Puritans, Tories and Whigs, Conservatives and Liberals, Conservatives and Labour. It is indeed true that, as we have seen, Conservative doctrine can be traced back to the Royalists and Labour doctrine to some, at least, of the doctrines of the Puritans. What is false, however, is the suggestion of institutional continuity. The duel has started afresh at intervals, with different duellists, and for different reasons. There is no continuous thread. Above all, though there has been at intervals a two-party conflict there was not until the nineteenth century a two-party system of government. The foundation of that system is the recognition that, when a party wins a general election, a Cabinet will be formed out of that party, that the Cabinet will accept the principle of collective responsibility to the House of Commons, and that opposing the Cabinet will be another party, accepting the principle of majority rule, but expecting sooner or later to replace the party in office and to form a Cabinet in its turn. These principles George III would not have understood. Indeed, they were not fully understood even by young Queen Victoria, though the Prince Consort saw the situation more clearly and advised her that Sir Robert Peel had to form a Conservative Government in 1841 because the Conservatives had won a majority at the general election of that year. In other words, the two-party system is less than 150 years old.

Having once been established, however, it tends to be self-perpetuating. The members of the party realise that their chance of office depends upon maintaining the unity of the party. This implies, first, that the leaders will not adopt a policy on which the party is acutely divided. By adopting Roman Catholic Relief in 1829, Wellington and Peel let in the Whigs and enabled them to reform the electoral law. By repealing the Corn Laws in 1846, Peel gave the Liberals an almost continuous period of office for 28 years. By adopting the policy of Home Rule in 1886, Gladstone kept the Conservatives in office (except for a short period in 1892–95) for 20 years. By repudiating Asquith's leadership in 1916, Lloyd George helped the Labour party to supplant the Liberal party as the alternative to the Conservative party. In each case there were other factors; but the lesson is plain, and indeed Disraeli drew it in his remarkable sketch of Sir Robert Peel's leadership.

The unity of the party implies, in the second place, the loyalty of party members to their leaders. Minority movements within a party are deprecated because they threaten to lead to disruption. 'Our men' must rally round their leaders because party divisions tend to 'let the other fellows in'. Only in extreme cases is rebellion justified. The Protectionists felt so strongly about the Corn Laws that they repudiated Peel. Joseph Chamberlain and the Whigs could not swallow Gladstone's brand of Home Rule. The conflict between Harcourt and Rosebery, which was also a conflict over imperialism, helped to destroy the Liberal Government of 1895. Winston Churchill left the Conservative party in 1904 over Free Trade, rejoined it in 1925, opposed Baldwin in the 'thirties, and came back into office only by the fortune of war. The Conservatives virtually ejected Balfour in 1911 and broke away from the Coalition, in spite of their leaders, in 1922. The Labour party split in 1931 over the problem of balancing the Budget in a financial crisis. These things do happen; unless the leaders are to become dictators within their respective parties they ought to happen from time to time. Party divisions are, however, dangerous to the political careers of those who bring them about, and they usually result in 'letting the other fellows in', perhaps for a long period.

This is perhaps the point to explain why this should be so. Experience suggests that few electors are induced to vote by a particular policy. Parties produce election programmes, and they probably gain a few votes. People do change their minds between the dissolution of Parliament and the ensuing general election. We must not, however, assume that they have always been influenced by electioneering. There is evidence that the change is often from nonconformity to conformity: the middle-class man who has been annoyed by the behaviour of the Conservative leaders decides that, after all, it is safer to vote Conservative; the trade unionist who intended to vote Conservative decides that, after all, he cannot vote for the 'bosses'. Perhaps even more often the change is from an intention not to vote to an intention to vote according to class interest, or from an intention to vote against class interest to an intention not to vote at all. The non-voters, it may be remarked incidentally, are very important people because in a British election, where opinion is fairly evenly balanced between the parties, the non-voters really decide the election. Had they voted for the one party or the other, that party would have won.

So far, however, we have assumed that electors tend to vote according to class interest: but this is not necessarily so. It is known that a very high proportion of electors, perhaps 80 per cent., vote the same way in successive elections. Partly, this is because of a continuing class interest; but partly, too, it is a compound of party loyalty and intellectual laziness. To most people an election is a passing interest, requiring less intellectual effort than a football pool. They tend, therefore, to adopt a point of view and to stick to it. Though the Liberal party has been a minority since 1923, there are still constituencies with a Liberal tradition. The Labour party gradually supplanted the Liberal party, not so much by converting Liberal electors as by attracting the young voters, so that the process took a whole generation. Indeed, the phenomenon of the 'swing of the pendulum' is very largely due to the continual process by which young electors are substituted for those who die. Having no party loyalties as yet, and accepting the view of the young that the 'old gang' is behaving stupidly, the young electors tend to vote against that party and so to determine their own political affiliations for a generation. What the parties try to do, of course, is to attract them by their youth organisations, to 'catch 'em young' and indoctrinate them.

These general tendencies must not be taken too rigidly. There are always numerous exceptions. In particular, there is always a substantial proportion of genuine 'floating voters', people whose minds really can be changed or made up by four years' experience of party government, or swayed by party programmes, or even affected by television, broadcasting, public meetings, leaflets and other types of electioneering. How numerous they are we do not know, for we cannot distinguish them from those voters who express doubts at the beginning of the election but eventually vote for the same old party, those electors who in fact never vote except on extreme provocation (as in 1931), and those electors who have never voted before (perhaps because they were too young) and are now in process of making up their minds. Probably the 'floating voters' are numerous enough to affect the results in marginal constituencies, i.e. those in which the parties are evenly balanced.

The 'swing of the pendulum' is remarkably uniform

throughout the country, though England tends to 'swing' more violently than Scotland and Wales. It is customary to express it in percentages of votes cast. Thus, if in 1955 the result in a constituency was:

Cholmondeley (C.)	25,000	(50%)
Jones (Lab.)	18,000	(36%)
Cadbury (Lib.)	7,000	(14%)
	50,000	

and in 1959 the result in that constituency was

Cholmondeley (C.)	22,000	(44%)
Jones (Lab.)	20,000	(40%)
Cadbury (Lib.)	8,000	(16%)
	50,000	

the 'swing' from Conservative to Labour[1] was

$$\tfrac{1}{2}[(50 - 44) + (40 - 36)] = 5\%.$$

This is a little misleading for four reasons. First, the method ignores the 'swing' to Liberal. Secondly, it pays no attention to the non-voters, who may have been considerable, for instance:

	1955	1959
Conservatives	25,000 (47·2)	22,000 (40·0)
Labour	18,000 (34·0)	20,000 (36·5)
Liberal	7,000 (13·2)	8,000 (14·5)
Non-voters	3,000 (5·6)	5,000 (9·0)
	53,000	55,000

Thirdly, the method ignores all cross-voting from one election to another. Finally, the percentage is misleading, since the Conservative wins not on his percentage but on his majority; and it is probably as easy to win 1000 votes in one con-

[1] I.e. half the Labour gain plus half the Conservative loss.

stituency as in another, though in the one it may be 3 per cent. and in another 10 per cent.

If we could analyse the votes more carefully, we should probably find that the result was somewhat as follows:

	1955		1959	
Conservative	25,000	Conservative	From Cons.	17,500
			From Lab.	1,000
			From Lib.	500
			From N.V.	500
			New	2,500
				22,000
Labour	18,000	Labour	From Cons.	2,000
			From Lab.	15,000
			From Lib.	500
			From N.V.	500
			New	2,000
				20,000
Liberal	7,000	Liberal	From Cons.	750
			From Lab.	500
			From Lib.	5,500
			From N.V.	250
			New	1,000
				8,000
Non-voters	3,000	Non-voters	From Cons.	1,500
			From Lab.	500
			From Lib.	500
			From N.V.	1,500
			New	1,000
				5,000
		Moved or Dead	From Cons.	2,000
			From Lab.	1,500
			From Lib.	500
			From N.V.	500
				4,500

This presents a very different picture, but it has not been deliberately distorted: it is the sort of thing that does happen. It shows (as indeed Mr D. E. Butler, who first put the 'swing' into this particular form, would readily admit) that the percentage 'swing' is at best a very rough approximation. It has to be used for two reasons. First, except in those rare constituencies in which sample polls are taken by private investigators, we know only the number of votes cast for each candidate and the total electorate. Secondly, in order to compare one constituency with another we have to use percentages. What is really significant is that, when the Conservative or Labour vote goes up or down in one constituency, it also goes up or down in nearly every other constituency. Further, when the number of non-voters goes up or down in one constituency, it goes up or down in most other constituencies. If the number of Liberal candidates remained the same in successive elections, we should be able to say that the pattern of change was the same in nearly every constituency. This arises from the homogeneity of the British electorate, so that the tendencies in the north of Scotland are similar to those in the south of England. What Mr Butler tried to do was to produce a formula for these tendencies. It is far from an accurate formula, but it does give a rough indication. Though the actual 'swing' is far more complicated than Mr Butler's hypothetical 'swing', it is nevertheless true that the electorate moves according to a pattern.

Why should this be so? First, the election is one of a long series of elections in which parties with long histories have sought the votes of electors, many of whom have long memories. Richard Roe's attitude to the Conservative party is not determined to any great extent by the personality of the present leader, for he remembers Mr Macmillan, Sir Anthony Eden, Sir Winston Churchill, Neville Chamberlain, Baldwin, Austen Chamberlain, Bonar Law, and perhaps Balfour; his father told him about Disraeli and his grandfather about Sir Robert Peel. Nor is Richard Roe's attitude determined to any great extent by the programme of the Conservative party in 1964. He remembers Suez, Munich, the crisis of 1931, the General Strike, Lloyd George's Coalition, perhaps even Home Rule. In other words, Richard Roe has a more or less permanent attitude to the Conservative party; and something quite startling has to happen before he changes his mind about it. The younger Richard Roe is, the less certain he is; though there is also evidence that electors tend to become more Conservative as they grow older. Even the young elector, however, does not consider party politics and party personalities entirely afresh. He has derived from his environment an 'image' of the Conservative party, a picture of its character. It may change as he grows older and more experienced. It is, however, generally true that electors vote for a party because, taking a very broad view, they think that party to be the 'best'.

This does not mean that policies and personalities are unimportant. The proportion of uncommitted electors at every election is large enough to give victory to either side. The 'image' which people have of a party is built up over long experience, so that if its policies are persistently unattractive or its personalities persistently weak it rapidly loses its reputation. Even a single event which arouses emotion, such as the General Strike, the Great Depression of 1931, the Hoare–Laval proposals of 1934, the Munich Agreement of 1938, and the Suez episode of 1956, has consequences over a long period. It forces individual electors to consider their politics; and many who do so become non-voters, or change to the other side.

The most important events, however, are those which cause a party to split. When Sir Robert Peel repealed the Corn Laws in 1846, a great many Conservatives agreed with him. Some, no doubt, eventually returned to the support of that party. On the other hand, enough Conservatives changed over to help the Liberals to keep a majority from

1846 to 1874. When the Liberal party split over Home Rule in 1886, enough Liberals became Liberal Unionists to prevent the Liberals from gaining a majority until 1906. Even in 1931 the Labour party permanently lost electors, though it gradually replaced them by young men and women, with the result that in 1945 it had a substantial majority.

Theoretically, the young men and women need not have supported Labour: they could have started a party of their own. Anybody can start a party, just as anybody can start a darts club or a football team. In many democratic systems parties spring up like mushrooms, for the very sensible reason that nobody except a party hack can possibly agree with every decision of any party—and also, perhaps, for the equally sensible reason that it is better to be leader of a small party than one of a multitude. In Britain, however, the purpose of a party is to win an election, and this means to win at least 320 seats. To win 320 seats one ought to have at least 500 candidates, and this would require 500 constituency associations. In each constituency there would have to be a considerable expenditure on office accommodation, a paid agent and election expenses (say £800 an election, not to mention local authority elections). At the centre there would have to be much expenditure on office accommodation, full-time staff, travelling expenses, conferences, propaganda, and so forth. It took the Labour party, with the financial resources of the trade unions behind it, forty-five years. Our young men and women might do it in a generation, though they would suffer severely from the competition of three existing parties. On the whole, it is easier for the young man or woman with political ambitions to join an existing party, mould its policy nearer to his (or her) own opinions, and achieve success in it. After all, obstreperous young men have got into the Cabinet in their second Parliament.

CHAPTER III

THE HOUSE OF COMMONS

1. POLITICAL AMBITION AND ITS REWARDS

Greville tells us that when Lord Melbourne was invited to become Prime Minister, 'he thought it a damned bore, and that he was in many minds what he should do—be Minister or no'. His private secretary protested: 'Why, damn it, such a position never was occupied by any Greek or Roman, and, if it only lasts two months, it is well worth while to have been Prime Minister of England.' 'By God, that's true,' replied Melbourne, 'I'll go.' It lasted not two months but, with a short interval, seven years. Nor did Melbourne's action at the time of the 'Bedchamber Plot' in 1839 suggest that he was anxious to leave. Naturally the post was more attractive than he had expected, since it fell to him to act as mentor to the young Queen Victoria. The story may not be true at all, but it is certainly true that 'it is well worth while to have been Prime Minister of England'.

Jokes are made about politicians in England as elsewhere; but the note of contempt and distrust which is evident in some countries is noticeably absent. If it is something to be Prime Minister, it is also something to be a member of Parliament. There is a prestige attached to the House of Commons. It has a dignity which it rarely forgets. It is the focus of attention when stirring events are on foot, and the place to which the ordinary individual looks when he thinks that 'something ought to be done' about his particular grievance. Political ambition not only is a virtue; it is commonly regarded as a virtue. A person does not soil his reputation by standing for election. It is not uncommon for individuals to choose a political career, not because money can be made out of it, but because 'it is something to have been Prime Minister', or even to have been a plain member of Parliament.

Political activity does not lead to wealth. The allowances of a member of Parliament amount to £3,250 a year, a small sum which, in many cases, covers little more than his personal expenses as a member. Hence, with some exceptions, a member has to have external sources of income—inherited or accumulated wealth, a profession, broadcasting or journalism, office in a trade union or co-operative society, etc. The highest paid political posts are those of the Prime Minister and the Lord Chancellor, who receive £14,000 a year. The former has heavy expenses to bear and the latter is at the top of a profession which is extremely remunerative for the few who achieve leadership. There is nothing to be gained by company promoting, as Labouchere in one of his most cynical remarks suggested that there was. There is no 'rake-off' from Government contracts, because members have no influence upon them. In short, the most that can be obtained is the consciousness of a job well done, the admiration of a multitude, the power to make history, some knowledge of confidential affairs and a peerage to sweeten one's declining years.

These are, however, attractive prizes, and it is right that they should be so. The nation requires to devote the service of its ablest members to its own cause. The task of governing is too difficult to be undertaken by the weak or the ignorant. Democratic States have to rely upon the efforts of the most intelligent, the most farsighted, and the most altruistic of each generation. It is by no means certain that the British Constitution succeeds in this task. We must ask at a later stage what particular qualities are required of a statesman. It must be recognised, however, that for most the path to office must be through the House of Commons, and the system of election is not operated in such a way as to secure in that House a sufficient reservoir of talent.

The difficulty lies in the House of Commons itself, which has made politics a matter for professionals but continues to pretend that it is a matter for amateurs. Of the great statesmen of the past hundred years, only a few had to earn their living—Disraeli wrote novels but he also married money; Asquith and Haldane practised at the Bar before they became full-time politicians; Morley and Winston Churchill were journalists and authors; Joseph Chamberlain and Bonar Law gave up their active concern with industry before they went into politics; Lloyd George tried to continue his practice as a solicitor, but later took to journalism when out of office. The professional politicians, living on inherited or accumulated wealth, were very much more numerous. On the other hand, in the nineteenth century there were on the back-benches many practising lawyers, stockbrokers, company directors, and other professional men who managed to take an active part in politics and yet to earn part at least of their income. The difficulties which have since developed are three. First, owing to the death duties introduced in 1894, together with high rates of tax on incomes, it is now much more difficult to accumulate, inherit or marry money. Secondly, official salaries have not kept pace with inflation and their real value has much diminished. A professional politician could hope that, once he had reached the level of a Parliamentary Secretary or Junior Lord of the Treasury, he would have on the average eight years in office and eight years out of it. If he had some private income, or if he had connexions which gave him directorships, or if he could earn enough by journalism, he could become a full-time politician while his party was in office and a part-time politician when it was in opposition. Nowadays, a Parliamentary Secretary finds it difficult to live on his income and there are many part-time politicians on the back-benches who cannot afford to take office.

Thirdly, the work of a conscientious member of Parliament has become so heavy that it is very difficult to earn an income. It is of course true that not all members are conscientious. The House begins sitting at 2.30 p.m. on four days a week, but the whips are careful to indicate the times of divisions, so that members need not always be in the House. There is a great deal of committee work to be done, some of it in the mornings; but some members are good at avoiding it and others put in a token attendance for half-an-hour or so. There is also much more constituency work—correspondence, meetings, 'clinics' (a new device whereby members agree to be in their constituency offices during stated periods in order to give advice to constituents who have grievances), social functions and so forth, have all increased. Britain differs from most democracies in that all members can visit their constituencies at weekends; and few feel justified in making visits less frequently than once a month.

Members of Parliament must therefore be drawn from limited classes of persons. In the first place they must be so interested in politics that they are prepared to spend a great deal of time in what is normally a very dull pursuit. History and the newspapers tell us of the moments of excitement, the 'scenes', the great debates. Only Hansard tells us about the great succession of extremely dull speeches; most of the committee work is not even recorded; and the dullest work of all, nursing a constituency, brings no reward save a few brief moments of glory, and perhaps a knighthood, a baronetcy or a peerage after a decade or two. Those who are willing to undertake this sort of job are obviously public benefactors, but they are a small section of the population.

In the second place, members of Parliament have usually to be drawn from people with rather superficial minds. The problem of Aden, for instance, is a difficult one, which takes a lifetime to master; so is the problem of the financing of contributory pensions. These are two problems out of several thousand problems for which the member of Parliament has to offer ready solutions. Many readers will have marvelled as they have seen members perform on television.

77

'Do the members favour a subsidy for British bacon?' The answer, we know, comes from the Conservative Central Office or Transport House (Labour party headquarters), but at least members have to know the answer, to be very learned about it, and to be equally learned about a thousand other subjects. Members have their specialities; but they have also to be knowledgeable about a vast number of subjects; and this requires a peculiar type of mind—the sort of mind which enjoys undergraduate debates.

In the third place, members must either have private incomes or be able to earn in part-time occupations. Many Conservatives, and some others, have both. Members receive allowances of £2,000 a year, subject to tax, and expense allowances free of tax (but they have to prove that the expenses have been incurred on parliamentary business) of £1250 a year. They also receive free transport for themselves between their constituencies and London. The rest—which may include the cost of two homes, one in London and one elsewhere, the cost of a car, secretarial expenses, contributions to charities in the constituency, and (every few years) personal expenses of something like £100 at a general election—has to be found by them.

The result is inevitable. On the Conservative side is a high proportion of *rentiers*, including most of the front-bench members, and also a considerable number of company directors, lawyers, accountants and other professional men practising in London. Most have been educated in fee-paying schools; and even self-made men are rare. In short, the Conservative party in Parliament—whatever be its strength outside—is drawn almost exclusively from the upper middle-class. The Parliamentary Labour party, on the other hand, contains a high proportion of trade union nominees—usually not the ablest trade union leaders because they are needed in the unions—who are subsidised by their unions. On the other hand, there are also many lawyers, journalists, broadcasters and others who find it possible to supplement their parliamentary salaries by means of part-time work. The middle-class element in the Labour party has been increasing since 1945.

On the other hand, it is no longer necessary for parliamentary candidates to find the cost of elections, other than their personal expenses, which by law may not exceed £100. Until late in the nineteenth century the whole cost of an election, including fees for officials and the erection of polling booths, fell on the candidates. Since 1884, these costs have been borne by local taxation; but it was still necessary for candidates to bear the expenses of their own organisation and propaganda. Even within the limits imposed by the Corrupt and Illegal Practices Act, 1883, the cost might be £1500 or £2000, apart from organisational expenses between elections, which might cost £500 per annum or more. These substantial sums were not necessarily found by the candidates themselves. Wealthy supporters were often willing to contribute to election funds; and pressure groups like railway companies, farmers' associations, etc., were sometimes prepared to guarantee the necessary funds by 'sponsoring' candidates. Nor was it unknown for Conservatives to contribute, as anonymously as possible, to the funds of working-class candidates, in the hope of 'splitting the Liberal vote'.

The development of the local association, with permanent funds, made easier the election of candidates who could not finance their own elections. Such an association could accept financial responsibility for the party candidate and raise the necessary funds. The number of constituency-financed candidates was, however, small until the Labour party was reorganised in 1918. Though that party allowed, and still allows, 'sponsoring' by trade unions, the Co-operative party, and other affiliated organisations, most of its candidates are financed by the constituency parties. The Conservative party has no 'sponsored' candidates, but organisations such as the National Farmers' Union and the National Union of Teachers provide funds for the election of

Conservative candidates under arrangements which are kept secret. Under the rules of the Conservative party, adopted after the general election of 1945, all Conservative candidates are financed by the constituency parties.

2. THE HOUSE AND THE GOVERNMENT

The fact that the essential difficulty of the House of Commons is the paucity of governmental talent shows the relative importance of the functions of the House. We should not think of criticising the United States House of Representatives because it contained few if any prospective Presidents. It is not a nursery for administrators but a legislative body. Under the British system, however, the Prime Minister is almost invariably a member of the House of Commons, and the majority of the Cabinet is also drawn from that House. The Government exists because it has a majority in the House. It is a party Government whose strength is determined by its maximum vote when the whips are put on. It is for that reason that a general election is a choice of Government. If it produces a Conservative majority, there will be a Conservative Government. If the party majority splits, there must be either a new Government or another general election.

The theory is that the House controls the Government. The Government, in the accepted phrase, is responsible to the House. In a very real sense the statement is accurate. It does not mean, however, that the House takes the proposals of the Government and moulds them according to its own wishes. Nor does it mean that the House gives instructions to the Government. It is equally true to say that the Government controls the House.

In normal circumstances the two-party system operates, and the Government has a homogeneous party majority. Sometimes the Government is a coalition and has to control two or three parties through their respective leaders. At other times, it has no majority, but has to collaborate with some other party—as Whigs collaborated with Peelites from 1846 to 1852, Conservatives with Liberal Unionists between 1886 and 1892, Liberals with the Labour party from 1910 to 1914 and the Labour Government with Liberals from 1929 to 1931. Where the support of another party is thus necessary, the leaders of that party have a large measure of control over the Government. The fact is that the leaders of a party are reasonably certain of their followers: and where the members of the Government are the leaders the Government controls a majority of the House.

Implicit in this statement is the assumption that the party obeys the whip. It is extraordinarily rare for it to fail to do so. It is not so much that party discipline is strict. Even in the Labour party the appearance of strictness is greater than the reality. It is true that a recalcitrant member may find himself deprived of his 'label' at the next election, and that it is the label which normally secures his return. In the Labour party, too, the label is presented by the National Executive Committee, by whom all 'official' Labour candidates must be approved. This sanction is, however, rarely necessary. The apparent strictness of the Labour party is due to the fact that, while the party is in Opposition, its attitude towards matters before the House is determined by weekly meetings of the whole parliamentary party and not, as in the other parties, by the leaders sitting in the 'Shadow Cabinet'. A Labour member who dissents is thus opposing a majority, and he is expected to do no more than abstain from voting. Also, the Labour party, like the old Liberal party, and indeed any progressive party, contains some political rebels and has therefore to exercise a more obvious control. Conservatives by definition do not go off on frolics of their own.

The truth is, though, that a member of the Government's majority does not want to defeat the Government. Normally he is loyal to his leaders, and to vote against them is to break faith not only with them but also with his constituents, who

81

elected him not because of his own opinions, nor because they thought that he was capable of exercising an independent judgment, but because he rendered allegiance to the party. They usually give him some latitude: but if he frequently votes against his own party he ought not to carry the party's label. The electors do not want men of independent views but good party men. They elected not Sir Richard Roe but the Conservative candidate.

Moreover it usually happens that the only way to vote against the Government is to vote with the Opposition. Frequently the question is so framed that the member cannot conscientiously do so. For instance, if a Conservative Government introduces a Bill to subsidise the pigskin industry, the Labour Opposition may perhaps move an amendment stating that, since the only way to reduce unemployment in the industry is to bring it under public control, the House declines to pass the Bill. If the member believes that *laissez-faire* is the correct policy for the pigskin industry, he cannot vote in either lobby. Even if the question were so framed as to enable dissident Conservatives to vote against the Government, they would hesitate. The Government has in its hands (or strictly, the Prime Minister has) the power of dissolving Parliament. If it is defeated it may prefer to 'appeal to the people' and not to 'bow to the will of the House'. The general election will cost members a great deal of effort; some of them may be defeated; and possibly the Government will be defeated and the Labour party will come into power. Or the Government may not dissolve, but resign, and so bring in a Labour Government. As between the deep blue sea on this side and the devil on the other, the average member naturally prefers the deep blue sea, and his conscience is usually pliable enough not to insist that he ought to drown himself.

This argument applies to all parties, and it follows that a defeat of the Government with a majority is very rare. Strictly speaking, no majority Government has been overthrown by a party split since Robert Lowe led 'the Cave of Adullam' against Gladstone's Reform Bill in 1866. There never was a majority for Home Rule in 1885, and there was no split in 1895 (when, in fact, the Government had no majority). But, because the Government is normally sure of its votes, it can treat any vote as a vote of confidence. The result is that (except on the rare occasions when the whips are not put on, or when a minority Government is in power) every vote is one of confidence. For an individual member to vote against the Government is thus to show lack of confidence in that Government. In other words, the question for the member is not whether he favours subsidies to pigskin manufacturers, but whether he supports the Government. The effect is cumulative. The majority votes for the Government, and therefore the Government controls the majority; because the Government controls the majority it insists on the votes of its majority. Cross-voting, except in minority parties, is rare.

This does not mean that the Government pays no attention to what is said in the House. It exists not because of the intelligence of its members or the excellence of its intentions, but because it won a majority at the last election. It will continue to exist only if it secures a majority at the next election. It will secure a majority only if its followers secure majorities or pluralities in their constituencies. Members must therefore sniff every breeze that blows, lest it develop into a gale that sweeps away enough votes to lose their seats. If any act of the Government threatens to lose votes, they will not vote against the Government in the lobbies but will complain to the whips in the smoking-room. A strong Government will resist pressure if it thinks that, ultimately, it can put its case and win: but the strongest Governments bow to the inevitable by gracefully acceding to the 'sense of the House'. It is because of this, as has already been emphasised, that we have Government by the people.

Nor is this all. Not all Government supporters are pliant

yes-men. They will not be beaten with whips and they wage war on ministerial scorpions. The House can be driven, but is far more easily led. A carrot may move a donkey when a dozen whips will not; and, after all, members of Parliament are intelligent animals. A way out must be managed, and management is often nothing more than an ability to make concessions gracefully.

It must be remembered, too, that members are not mere representatives of their constituents. The association of Labour members with trade unions and co-operative societies has already been mentioned. The close connection between other members and other bodies known generally in America as 'pressure groups' is less well understood. When the Labour Government consulted the Trades Union Congress, its opponents spoke of 'outside dictation'; but the language of opposition must not be adopted too easily. The connection between the Conservative party and the Drink Trade is perhaps less close than it was before 1914. It was due to the close association of Nonconformity, 'Temperance', and the Liberal party of the nineteenth century. 'The Trade' has never recovered from the combination of Mr Lloyd George's restrictions, the attractions of Hollywood, and television; high prices and sex appeal have driven men from drink, and though the public-house has lost no profits its political influence has declined. Besides, women now have votes. There are, however, hosts of pressure groups, of which the National Farmers' Union and the Institute of Directors are among the most successful. In our Constitution these groups seek to act upon the Government because privileges come from the Government even if they pass by way of the House. It is wise, however, to provide for bringing up reserves, and most pressure groups have unpaid representatives in the House. Nor need they be in one party only. Where extra profits are sought they must necessarily be obtained through parties that do not treat profit as sin; but where what is wanted are better conditions for public employees, better social services, or 'justice' for little men, it is better to secure representation in all parties.

Consequently, the member for Casterbridge may also be member for the National Union of Pigskin Manufacturers or the National Association of Public Stenographers. When a question affecting his second constituency is before the House, he is provided with a brief which needs only a few 'Mr Speaker's' to become a valuable and informed contribution. He states publicly what has already been urged upon the minister privately. If a concession will gain a few votes, or if administration will become easier if the goodwill of the association is obtained, or if the request for 'justice' is not ill-founded, the minister will concede gracefully in the House what he has already accepted outside. Indeed, the honourable member's speech may bring to the minister's attention an argument which hitherto had stopped much lower in the official hierarchy. In any case, the glory will go to the honourable member, who will naturally receive the gratitude and applause of the association at its next annual dinner.

Nor must it be thought that members without axes to grind cannot produce useful amendments. In spite of the thorough preparation which nearly every Bill receives in the Government Departments, all legislation, because of its general character, tends to produce anomalies. These are sometimes discovered by private members, or discovered by the draftsmen because members are puzzled. Consequently, most large Bills receive some amendments produced, directly or indirectly, by private members, especially now that nearly all Bills are examined in small Standing Committees.

It must not be forgotten, though, that the last word as well as the first rests with the Government. The major legislation enacted by Parliament is the Government's legislation. The external policy of the nation is the Government's policy. Taxation is imposed by Parliament but determined by the Chancellor of the Exchequer. The Government not only proposes but, through its majority, disposes. Even so, it is not the Government standing alone. It is the Government in Parliament. It is a Government, too, whose only authority is the support of public opinion witnessed for the time being by its majority in the House of Commons. Its policy must in the near future be submitted to the people. The axe will fall upon those who lose touch with public opinion: and the longer the blow is parried the more heavily it will fall—as the Conservatives discovered in 1906.

It cannot be said that this is dictatorship. At worst it is dictatorship for a term of years certain; but dictators who at short intervals have to beg the people for votes freely cast are the servants of the public and not its masters. Those who regret the snows of yester year do not realise that yester year was long ago when the great landowners governed *en société anonyme*. Government is too complicated a business to be conducted by 630 persons in open debate. It requires the whole apparatus of study and execution which is described in Chapter VI. Behind every proposal is a great collection of files, a long series of committee meetings, a large number of individual discussions and, indeed, the whole mechanism of administration. Parliament cannot govern. It can do no more than criticise. Moreover, we have discussed these questions in terms of the majority. Facing the Government Front Bench is the Opposition Front Bench. There is no dictatorship so long as there is an Opposition.

3. THE OPPOSITION

If Parliament's main function is to criticise, the Opposition is its most important part. Its members are, so to speak, critics by profession. It has often been pointed out that the House of Commons, unlike most other legislatures, has its seats arranged not in a semi-circle, but facing each other in two large blocks separated by a gangway. To the right of the Speaker are the Government and its supporters: to the left is the Opposition. There is no gradation from right to left, but a clear division. A member who gradually loses faith in the Government cannot proceed by easy stages; he must wait until he is ready to take the great decision to 'cross the floor'. It is true that there are more subtle distinctions. A minister who resigns because he disagrees with the Government's policy speaks from a seat 'below the gangway' which separates the Treasury bench from the benches further away from the Speaker. The leader of a minority party similarly speaks from 'below the gangway' on the Opposition side. Fundamentally, however, the topography of the House recognises the stark division of the two-party system.

The members of the Government sit on the front bench to the right of the Speaker and the leaders of the Opposition on the front bench to his left. Opposite the Cabinet, therefore, is the 'Shadow Cabinet' (though it is not officially so called in the Labour Party): opposite Her Majesty's Government is Her Majesty's Opposition. It is a strange name, first used in jest; yet it is so expressive that it has become almost official. The Opposition is Her Majesty's alternative Government: only a small change in voting at the next election is necessary to induce Government and Opposition to change places. Leaders of the Opposition and the Chief Whips in both Houses have salaries, charged on public funds, so that they may exercise their functions without the distraction of earning a living.

This fact shows more plainly than anything else that opposition is regarded as an essential part of the Constitution. The British Constitution not only does not expect conformity, it demands the opposite. The Government has its majority and so can govern; but it must do so under a constant fire of criticism from the Opposition. Opinion outside is assumed to be divided; therefore it is desirable that inside the House ministers may be reminded of Cromwell's injunction: 'I beseech you, in the bowels of Christ, think it possible that you may be mistaken.' Nor can ministers forget that politically they are mortal. What the Opposition says may be so persuasive that the 'floating vote' may 'swing the pendulum'. Ministers must answer argument by argument; they must meet a half-truth by a whole truth (or a more attractive half-truth) lest it run round the country. In this way the appeal to the people is not an occasional ceremony, but a process which goes on daily and hourly in the parliamentary session.

No doubt opposition delays the process of government. Between 1 and 7 September 1939 Parliament passed enough legislation to occupy two or three sessions, because the Opposition agreed not to oppose. In war time a Government expects and receives power to legislate by Order in Council because enemies do not travel at the speed of the democratic process. It must be remembered, however, that we demand not only action but just action—action that is subjected to public approval or disapproval. Nor is the delay so great as might appear, because the administrative process also is long, and it is prepared while legislation is in Parliament.

Frequently, too, debate embarrasses the Government. How easy it would be for the Government to ride off after a blunder if it had not to meet the criticism which inevitably follows. Negotiations with foreign powers are difficult to conduct when a lynx-eyed Opposition sits suspiciously on the watch. We might have a better foreign policy if we had no Parliament: but we might have a worse; and what is better and what is worse is generally a matter of opinion. We are a free people because we can criticise freely and, if our criticisms prove persuasive, compel the Government to withdraw. Public opinion has destroyed a good many Bills and has reversed a good many policies. The spear-head of the attack is the Opposition. To find out whether a people is politically free it is necessary only to ask if there is an Opposition and, if there is, to ask where it is.

All this assumes, of course, that the House debates in public. Government and Opposition speak to each other, but for the education of the people. The criticisms brought against the Government are the criticisms of ordinary individuals; the answers of the Government are formally answers to the Opposition, but substantially they are replies to the questions raised in the factory, the railway carriage and the office. The members of the House of Commons were not elected for their special qualifications, but because they supported the policies which the majority of their constituents were prepared to accept. They have no authority except as representatives, and in order that their representative character may be preserved they must debate in public. Secret sessions were suited to the oligarchic government of the eighteenth century. They are the negation of democratic principles. No doubt there are exceptional occasions when secrecy is justified. Compulsory military service was until recently contrary to the British tradition. In 1916 it was considered necessary in the interest of the community to propose compulsory enlistment. In normal times a change so great could not be effected without a 'mandate' from the people obtained by including the proposal in a party manifesto at a general election. In 1916 it was impossible to have a general election. What is more, it was impossible, without giving information of great value to the enemy, even to explain the reasons fully in public. On the other hand, no Government should be trusted to make so great a change without detailed explanation. It was therefore necessary that the explanation should be made in a secret session. The procedure was justified by the exceptional conditions. There were similar conditions in the war of 1939–45 and the need for secrecy was on occasions so obvious that open debate was dangerous. The number of secret sessions suggested, however, that members were mistaking their functions. They appeared to think that, as members, they had something particular to contribute to the conduct of the war, that their views on military strategy or foreign policy were of more value than those of Tom, Dick or Harry. The truth is that they were Tom, Dick and Harry. They were not elected to contribute special knowledge or special ability to the conduct of affairs; they were chosen because they were ordinary people capable of representing ordinary people. Their functions, as Mr Greenwood correctly stated at the outbreak of war, were to bring the views of ordinary people to the attention of the Government and to act as channels through which explanations could be given to ordinary people by the Government.

Even in normal times, it is not the business of an Opposition to obstruct government. Its purpose is to criticise, not to hinder. There are no doubt exceptional circumstances where obstruction is permissible. Given the assumptions of the Irish Nationalist party before 1914, no blame for obstruction can properly be laid against them. Their concern was not to make the Union workable but to destroy it. Moreover, where a Government is forcing a policy on the country which it is reasonably certain that the country does not approve, the Opposition may reasonably demand that it be submitted to the people. It is not so easy to interpret this principle. The Government naturally reads the signs one way and the Opposition another. For instance, the Conservative Opposition obstructed the Parliament Bill in 1911 and Home Rule in 1912. The Liberal Government had a majority after 1910 only with Labour and Irish support. The Conservatives therefore said that the Liberals had a mandate for neither, because the Irish voted for the Parliament Bill to secure Home Rule, and Great Britain had produced a majority against both. Whether the 'predominant partner' alone had a right to determine the course is a question of opinion. It should be said, however, that a party which proposes to use its majority while in power should accept a majority verdict against it. Obstruction brings parliamentary government into contempt, and it is both politically wise and constitutionally sound not to over-emphasise lawyers' arguments about 'mandates'. If a Government offends public opinion by a too extensive use of its power, the Opposition will reap the benefit.

Remedies have, however, been devised to meet obstruction. It is no longer possible to 'talk out' a proposal by lengthy speeches and much repetition. When the Speaker or Chairman considers that enough has been said, the Chief Whip or any other member can move that 'the question be now put' and so use the party majority to closure the debate. A multiplicity of amendments can no longer be moved because the Speaker or Chairman has power to 'select' those which appear to raise the essential issues—a power known as the 'kangaroo'. Finally, if it appears that the debate on a Bill will be long, the Government can always move a 'guillotine' resolution to closure the debate by compartments—to allot, that is, so many hours to the discussion on each stage and each group of sections.

These devices add to the power which the Government possesses by virtue of its majority. Indeed, the closure and the guillotine can be used only where the majority obeys the whip. Great though the power is, the Government recognises the right and the duty of the minority to criticise. It must do so, for an attempt to 'gag' could be represented as arising from a recognition of administrative failure and would be a powerful argument in favour of the Opposition. It is therefore natural that parliamentary proceedings should in the main be regulated by what are politely called 'the usual channels' which are said to pass 'behind the Speaker's Chair' —in other words, by negotiations between the two or three sets of whips.

Private members are allowed to move motions and to debate Bills introduced by them only on about twenty Fridays (when the sittings are short) during the session. Even here the whips are not without influence, because often private members (who have to draw lots for the opportunity) are called upon suddenly to produce Bills and motions, and if their powers of rapid invention of grievances are not good, it is natural for them to seek the advice of the whips. Members sometimes produce their own ideas, and sometimes ideas elaborated by pressure groups; but often a motion or a Bill comes not from the private member's head but from the whips' pigeon-holes.

This is, however, a very small proportion of the business of the House; the rest of the time is taken up by Government business. The time covers, in fact, four full days a week up to about Whitsuntide, and the whole week of five days thereafter. Also, it needs only a majority vote, proposed by the Government, to deprive private members of their time altogether. It is the Government business which is arranged with the Opposition. Every Thursday the Leader of the Opposition asks the Prime Minister what is the business for the coming week. He knows the answer already, because the two of them have arranged it through the whips: but this is a convenient method of informing the House. The Government has a rough plan for the session, arranged by the Legislation Committee of the Cabinet. It brings up the business in the order convenient to itself; but there is a good deal of leeway. There are, for instance, twenty-six 'Supply days' for debating Estimates, Supplementary Estimates, etc. It does not matter in what order they are taken. If the Opposition wishes to attack the Government's foreign policy, the Chief Whip offers to have the Foreign Office vote put down for Tuesday, provided that the Opposition will allow the Committee stage of the Pigskin Industry (Reorganisation) Bill to be completed on Monday. It is so agreed, and on Tuesday the Foreign Secretary moves the Foreign Office vote and puts the Government's case. The 'Shadow Minister' for Foreign Affairs on the Opposition side then attacks the Government and perhaps moves to reduce the vote because of the dangerous and vacillating policy of the Government. The debate ebbs and flows across the gangway until, at about 9 p.m., another front-bench speaker on the Opposition side 'catches the Chairman's eye'. It happens that about 9.30 p.m. the Minister of State in the Foreign Office catches the Chairman's eye and, strange to relate, he runs out of arguments just before 10 o'clock, when the House must adjourn, and it appears that no other member wishes to speak. The Opposition amendment is put to the vote and is, of course, lost. Probably, the Foreign Secretary will now ask leave to withdraw his motion, because the Opposition may want to attack the Government's foreign policy on another day. The surprising orderliness of this procedure is not surprising at all, because it was all arranged by the whips beforehand.

Nor is this an isolated example. It is part of the ordinary procedure. When this is made clear, some people denounce the whole thing as a sham, especially if they regard the Government as the tools and the Opposition as the dupes of some mysterious, nefarious and most able people known as 'the Capitalists'. It is, however, an exhibition of the logic of the democratic system. The Government must govern and the Opposition must oppose; what is more desirable than that they should arrange for their functions to be exercised in the best and most orderly fashion? The Government has power to obstruct opposition, and the Opposition has power to obstruct government: but neither kind of obstruction is desirable. Confusion will result if both make the attempt; and if one of them does, it will get a black mark in many an elector's register.

The efficiency of this system of government by cross-talk depends on the ability of the House to find able and acceptable chairmen. Nothing exhibits so well the genius of the British Constitution or, more accurately, the reasonableness of British people, as the position occupied by Mr Speaker. He is chosen by the Government from the Government benches when there is a vacancy. Invariably, however, the Opposition is consulted, and its veto is usually conclusive. He is intended to be as impartial as any human being can be. Accordingly, he must be chosen from among those members who have not made themselves conspicuous by the virulence of their politics. Often he has served a long apprenticeship as Chairman or deputy Chairman of Ways and Means, so that he may for many years have presided over the House in committee, or over the House itself during the Speaker's absence. Before that he may have been one of the members of the Chairmen's panel, selected by the Speaker from all parties to preside over Standing Committees and to act as temporary Chairman of the House when occasion arises. It is by no means uncommon for a Standing Committee with a Government majority to be presided over by a member of the Opposition. In the exercise of his functions he does not hesitate to overrule a minister. Nor does the minister hesitate to accept the ruling. The House has long ago realised that it can do nothing unless it has good chairmen. It has, therefore, deliberately exalted their status. A member of the Chairmen's panel and a Chairman of Ways and Means share in the great prestige of the Speaker.

That prestige is maintained with all the art which the British Constitution knows so well how to employ. Outside Parliament, Mr Speaker is for ceremonial purposes the House of Commons. His election is rarely opposed in his constituency. Inside the precincts but outside the Chamber forms and ceremonies support his dignity. He is preceded by the Sergeant-at-Arms carrying the successor of 'that bauble' which Cromwell ordered to be removed. His procession moves through the corridors to the call of 'Speaker', and in the central lobby his coming is notified by the command 'Hats off, strangers!' Standing at the bar of the House of Lords it is he who acts as 'House of Commons' when the Queen or her Commissioners sit 'in Parliament'. Inside the House his word is law. His rising is a signal for the member 'holding the floor' to sit. He insists that he, and not other members, be addressed. He requires that members do not cross between him and the member speaking. Members bow to him as they leave the Chamber. The importance of these apparently empty ceremonies must be emphasised because, though they often make ardent reformers impatient, they really have a purpose. It is natural and pardonable that a new member should despise this 'mummery', which appears to him to be intended to prevent him from discussing fully and adequately the empty stomachs, the lice, the leaking roofs, and the rest, that induced him to become a politician. It is, however, part of the process of enabling that member to put his case. Other members dispute the causes and may deny the facts. Debates on subjects on which political passion runs high is possible only if it is conducted with dignity and decorum. The ceremonies which attend Mr Speaker assist in creating that 'atmosphere' which is so potent in making the parliamentary system workable. Order is the primary requisite of freedom.

It must not be assumed that parliamentary procedure represents the highest degree of wisdom. It is always undergoing development, but here as elsewhere reforms are apt to come tardily. A discussion of present difficulties would involve an examination of rules and practices of a technical order which would be out of place in this book. It may be said, however, that the problem lies in the apparent contradiction between two demands, for speed on the one hand and full and comprehensive discussion on the other hand. It is not possible to have both. Most of the recent reforms have emphasised speed and have therefore met with criticism because they limited discussion.

CHAPTER IV

THE HOUSE OF LORDS

I. A CONSERVATIVE BULWARK

The House of Lords shares with the Corporation of the City of London the privilege of having passed almost unscathed through the 'reform' movement which began about 1782 and developed with great vigour after 1830. The reason is not that there has been universal satisfaction with its work. Indeed, dissatisfaction has gradually extended to all parties. There is now agreement that changes are necessary; but the problem as to what these changes shall be lies near the centre of political controversy. The House of Lords is for practical purposes an outpost of the Conservative party, though the peers possess a greater freedom of action than the Conservative members in the House of Commons. Changes made under a Conservative Government are hardly likely to prove acceptable to its successors, and changes could not be made under any other Government without a controversy between the two Houses.

The Conservative party has an immense majority because, subject to all the qualifications which have already been set out, the division between the parties is in essence a class division and the peers are drawn almost exclusively from one class. Indeed, the gradual 'Conservatisation' of the House is one of the means of showing that the party division is, in large measure, an economic division. So long as Whigs disputed with Tories, the party strength among the peers depended primarily on which party had been longest in office. In 1712 the Whigs had a majority, and the Tory Government created twelve new peerages in order to pass the Treaty of Utrecht. In 1832 the long period of Tory government—practically from 1784 to 1830—gave the Tories a majority of about fifty. The Whigs were in office from 1830 to 1841, and from 1846 (with two short intervals) until 1866. About 1865 the two parties were fairly evenly balanced. At least since 1832 there had been a tendency for traditionally Whig families to become Conservative, because the Liberal party was the party of reform, the party whose strength lay among dissenting manufacturers and not among Anglican land-owners. The tendency was offset by the creation of new peerages under Liberal Governments. However, the associa-tion of liberalism and radicalism under Gladstone after the second Reform Act caused the movement to become much more rapid. In 1886 the Whigs parted company with the Liberals over Home Rule: only forty-one peers voted for the second Home Rule Bill in 1893. In 1911 it would have been necessary to create five hundred peers to secure the passage of the Parliament Bill. The rise of the Labour party com-pleted the process. Of the peers who take a whip, the Con-servative peers outnumber the Labour peers by something like thirteen to one.

Whatever their political opinions, however, peers are responsible to nobody save themselves. Whether of the first or the fourteenth generation they take their seats by their own right. They need no labels. They take the whip because they desire it, not because they require it. No jealous con-stituency watches their votes or notes how assiduously they attend to their duties. They have not to trim their sails to the breezes of public opinion. They can decide as their reason or their private interest indicates. Consequently, Conservative peers are usually more conservative than the Conservative party. They have not, as the Conservative party has, to prove to working-class and lower middle-class people that Con-servatism is the best policy for all classes. In the party sense they need not be good Conservatives.

Nevertheless, a Conservative Government is always quite certain of its majority. It may have to grant concessions in the House of Lords as in the House of Commons. It must not antagonise the landowners, the City of London, or the whisky interest. They are, after all, representative of important political groups, and some of them probably contribute substantially to party funds. This is, however, a question of 'management' differing not fundamentally from that in the House of Commons. No Bill promoted by a Conservative Government has been rejected by the House of Lords since 1832; and, for the last eighty years, at least, no Conservative Bill has been amended against firm Government opposition.

The position of other Governments is quite different. Not many peers attend—rarely more than two hundred, and usually not more than eighty—but among them is always a Conservative majority. This majority usually obeys the commands of its leaders, though sometimes it has defeated the Government when its leaders suggested that it should not. The leaders themselves determine their strategy in consultation with the Conservative leaders in the House of Commons. Nothing passes the House of Lords except by permission of the Conservative party, whether that party is in office or in opposition.

This does not mean that no Liberal or Labour legislation passes the House of Lords. For the Conservative peers to adopt such tactics would be to invite the destruction of their privileges. Moreover, as we shall see presently, the House of Lords can now (since 1911) be overriden on any public Bill which is not a Bill to extend the maximum duration of Parliament. This power has altered both the strategy and the tactics of Conservative peers. Even before 1911, however, they had to exercise their power according to some principle which could be defended by Conservative politicians in the country. They exercised what Lord John Russell in 1839 called 'a wise discretion' and claimed to reject legislation only when it did not appear clearly that it had the support of the country. Even if this principle were honestly applied, it would assume that Conservative peers, who never fought an election, were better judges of public opinion than those who had to persuade a majority of the electors to support them at intervals. In practice, however, the principle was a mere excuse. Public opinion had little to do with it. The real reason was a combination of honest opinion and party tactics. The House naturally passes Bills of which it does not disapprove. It passes other Bills if it is tactically wise to do so. It radically amends if it considers that the Government would prefer a mutilated Bill to no Bill at all, or if it is tactically less dangerous to amend than to reject. It used to reject if the Conservative party was prepared to risk an election, or if it was believed that the Government would acquiesce without a dissolution. Rejection is now rare because it is, generally, ineffective.

Lord Balfour once said, while he was leader of the Unionist party, that it was the bounden duty of his audience to see that 'the great Unionist party should still control, whether in power or whether in Opposition, the destinies of this great Empire'. No such claim is now made, though sometimes Conservatives assume that the House of Lords ought to halt measures of a radical nature until the 'mind of the country' has been made up. Though most Conservatives agree that the House of Lords needs reform, they do not always accept the argument that it needs reform because it is Conservative. Every Conservative plan of reform so far put forward would give a Conservative majority. Nor are they necessarily thinking of party advantage. In their view, the Liberal and Labour parties often advocate rash and immature plans of social reform which, if carried out, would be dangerous to the peace and economic stability of the country. Such plans may be superficially attractive to the electorate, particularly if they are accompanied by wild promises of future benefit. They may be sprung suddenly on the electorate at a general election; or they may be so wrapped up in a multitude of proposals that their significance may not be plain. They may even be carried through the House of Commons without having been part of an election programme. Further, a

Government with a majority in the House of Commons has not necessarily a majority in the country. It may never have had such a majority, or it may have lost it long before the Parliament comes to an end. Finally, a majority for a Government is not necessarily a majority for every specific proposal made by the Government.

Some of these arguments apply to a Conservative Government as to a Labour or Liberal Government. A Conservative Government does not, however, propose 'rash' or 'revolutionary' or 'radical' measures. Consequently, a Labour or Liberal Government requires a Conservative brake, while a Conservative Government is, so to speak, a slow-moving vehicle which is never likely to get out of control. Hence, it is argued, a Conservative majority in the Second Chamber is very desirable, so long as it exercises its powers reasonably, as most Conservatives allege that it has done for the past century. The only reform required is in the composition of the majority, and most Conservative schemes of reform provided for a substantial reduction in the number of hereditary peers sitting in the House and for the addition of life peers or of 'Lords of Parliament' elected by the House of Commons.

It will be seen that some of the arguments could be met by a more accurate system of political representation in the House of Commons, though it was Conservative members who defeated such proposals in 1918 when the peers supported them, and the Conservative party has always refused to adopt them. Other arguments depend upon a fundamental suspicion of democracy based on a wide franchise. Moreover, the whole assumes that a Conservative majority will always act reasonably. There is very little basis for such an assumption. Sweet reasonableness is no more a Conservative characteristic than it is a Labour or Liberal characteristic. All power is likely to be abused unless it is adequately checked. The power of the House of Commons is checked by the ultimate power of the electorate. Sharp practices of the kind which Conservatives fear reap their reward at the next election, as was discovered by the Conservatives after the 'khaki' election of 1900, by Mr Lloyd George after the 'Hang the Kaiser' election of 1918, and by the Conservatives after the 'Red letter' election of 1924. The misuse of the prerogative of dissolving Parliament in 1900 was followed by the enormous 'swing' of 1906, though not all of it was due to the 'khaki' election. Mr Lloyd George's similar attempt to cash in on the feeling of gratitude and relief at the end of the war in 1918 gained him the support of a great array of the 'hard-faced' Conservatives, who turned him out in 1922; and he never again obtained office. The 'Red Letter', which helped the Conservatives to win a majority in 1924 could still be used, forty years later, to blunt the edge of Conservative propaganda. It is a fallacy to assume that, because a Government has a majority in the House of Commons it can do what it pleases. Though every Parliament passes laws which would not be accepted by the electorate as separate proposals, the Government's general tendency must be in accord with public opinion lest it be thrown out of office for a decade. Nor is there any cause to fear the electorate. The average elector has more sound common sense than he is commonly given credit for. He is not swayed by oratory, and he takes all electioneering with a pinch of salt. He is essentially conservative because in our social system he fears the consequence of extensive changes. In truth, politicians at the other extreme are equally mistaken in their political psychology. The political organisers of the Labour party have discovered by experience that the 'inevitability of gradualism' is a law applying to elections as well as to administration. The trade unions are suspicious of 'intellectuals' who want to do too much too quickly; and even if the Labour party adopted truly revolutionary proposals, the only result would be that even more substantial sections of the working class would vote Conservative. What is more, no election can be won by the votes of the industrial workers alone. The lower middle class, which holds the balance, is the most conservative and most timid section of the population. It fears change because things might be worse. It does not follow that the present tendency to transfer capital from the wealthy to the State will not continue; but if the argument is that the wealthy classes ought to be protected, it leads to the conclusion that what is required is a dictatorship, not a Conservative majority in the House of Lords. If we want a democracy we must inevitably trust the people.

2. THE NEED FOR A SECOND CHAMBER

An argument that the House of Lords ought not to have a permanent Conservative majority is not necessarily an argument that there ought not to be a House of Lords. It would not be impossible to provide a Second Chamber giving a better representation of national interests and aspirations. The question whether such a Chamber is desirable depends on the functions which the House of Lords performs or could perform.

It must be remembered that the House performs some functions which are not usually given to a Second Chamber. It is, for instance, the final Court of Appeal for many legal causes arising in the United Kingdom. It was intended in 1873 to abolish this jurisdiction and legislation was passed for the purpose; but as a result of a change of Government the decision was reversed and the legislation repealed. Instead, authority was given for the appointment of paid 'Lords of Appeal in Ordinary' who hold life peerages and sit in the House of Lords as ordinary members. The House of Lords for judicial business is in reality, though not in law, a different body from the House of Lords for legislative business, and it would be possible to abolish the latter without abolishing the former.

In the second place, the House debates general issues of policy. These debates are often very good. They are short, and few peers take part. Those who do are generally the peers with experience as minister, governor-general, ambassador, or otherwise. There are silly speeches in the House of Lords as in the House of Commons: but a peer rarely speaks for the sake of speaking. There is no necessity to 'keep the debate going'; there are no constituents to demand frequent intervention; there are no great advantages to be obtained from publicity. Moreover there is usually no division at the end; and if there is it does not matter, because the Government pays no attention whether to victory or to defeat. On the other hand, with the present House most of the debate is on one side if it is carried on for very long, because neither the Labour nor the Liberal party has more than a handful of speakers. These debates are useful but not essential. If the House were more representative they might be even more useful. In this respect, then, there would be some loss if the House were abolished.

In the third place, the House acts as a legislative chamber. Bills can be introduced there instead of in the House of Commons. The Bryce Committee stated in 1918 that Bills dealing with subjects of a partially non-controversial character may have an easier passage through the House of Commons if they have been fully discussed and put into a well-considered shape before being submitted to it. Government Bills ought, of course, to be in a well-considered shape before they are submitted to Parliament at all. It is nevertheless true that many amendments are made after publication because of representations made by 'pressure groups' and other interested parties. The amendments are proposed by the Government, and in such cases the House of Lords merely ratifies them. Occasionally, also, useful amendments are suggested by peers—the 'law lords', for instance, sometimes secure improvements in measures of law reform. Generally, however, peers do not give the close attention to public Bills which members of the House of Commons give in Standing Committee, and many proposed amendments are simply 'party political'. When a Liberal or Labour Government is in power the result is to increase the time occupied in legislation in the House of Commons. Nevertheless, the statement of the Bryce Committee is substantially correct, though no great emphasis must be placed upon it. Bills are sometimes introduced by peers. They are comparatively rare, because the British Parliament has long ago learned that its task is primarily to criticise legislative proposals, not to initiate them. They cannot pass the Commons unless they are entirely non-controversial or are supported by the Government: but occasionally a Bill presented by a peer does get through.

Fourthly, the House of Lords debates Bills brought up from the House of Commons. This is the function in the exercise of which the House of Lords has most laid itself open to attack. Before 1911 the only remedy available to a Liberal Government was to threaten to create enough peers to give the Government a majority. Obviously the threat could be used only in extreme cases. It was used in 1712 to pass the Treaty of Utrecht, in 1832 to pass the Reform Bill, and in 1911 to pass the Parliament Bill. It was such an extreme remedy that it could be used only where the monarch could be definitely assured that the measure had popular support; it thus demanded a preliminary general election and its use obstructed all business for several months.

In 1911, however, the Parliament Act gave a simpler remedy. The occasion for that Act was the rejection by the House of Lords of the Finance Bill of 1909 which gave effect to Mr Lloyd George's 'confiscatory' land-tax Budget. The House had never before refused to pass a Finance Bill and it was alleged that to do so was to infringe the privilege of the House of Commons to be the sole judge of financial measures (though, apart from history, there is no compelling reason why a money Bill should be treated differently from any other Bill). Accordingly, the Parliament Act enabled a money Bill to be presented for the royal assent and become law if it was not passed by the House of Lords within one month of its receipt. Conservative criticisms have propagated the notion that this provision creates a very wide breach in the power of the peers. It is said, for instance, that socialist provisions can be 'tacked' to a money Bill. Actually, the term 'money Bill' is very strictly defined, and it has been very rigidly interpreted by successive Speakers. The accusation really is that in a Labour Parliament Mr Speaker might be so biased as to allow tacking; but all history is against partial Speakers, and there is no more reason for Mr Speaker to demean the high traditions of his office than there is for a judge to do so. Somebody, somewhere, must take the decision; and Mr Speaker has the advantage of a thorough knowledge of parliamentary procedure and the practice of legislation.

The provision as to money Bills is thus of comparatively minor importance. It really covers the Consolidated Fund Bills which grant money to the Crown (and which are never amended by the House of Commons), certain other minor Bills which are rarely controversial, and less than half of the Finance Bills which impose taxation. It will be noted, however, that for this branch of legislation we have in practice single-chamber government.

In respect of other public Bills (except Bills to extend the maximum duration of Parliament) the House of Lords could after 1911 interpose a delay of two years. In the meantime the Bill had to pass the House of Commons in three successive sessions. Though this seemed not unreasonable in 1911, when the legislation contemplated dealt with such matters as Home Rule for Ireland and the disestablishment of the Welsh Church, the rise of the Labour party produced a demand for rapid social reform, which two years' delay would seriously obstruct. A Labour Government came into office in August 1945 with a programme which was large but, considering that it had been out of office (except as part of a coalition) for 14 years, not excessive. A good deal of legislation on social services had been prepared under the Coalition Government and was acceptable, with comparatively small changes, to the Labour Government: it occupied most of the session 1945–46. Meanwhile orders were given for the preparation of Bills to give effect to the major items of the party's election policy. By strict use of the guillotine, these were passed in 1946–47 and 1947–48. The only major item of policy not covered by October 1948 was the nationalisation of iron and steel. This was an exceedingly complicated proposal which involved much preparation. It could hardly have been completed earlier or passed through Parliament if it had been completed. At the end of the 1947–48 session, however, the Parliament had less than two years to run. The Parliament Act did not require that the three sessions should all be in the same Parliament; but the Labour Government wished to be able to appeal to the people in the later months of 1949 or in the early months of 1950 with the assertion that the 'mandate' expressed in 1945 had been fully carried out. This could be done only if the period laid down by the Parliament Act was reduced from two years to one year, and such a change could be effected (against the House of Lords) only by a Bill under the Parliament Act. The Parliament Act, 1949, therefore reduced the period from two years to one year and the number of sessions from three to two. Hence any public Bill (other than a Bill to extend the maximum duration of Parliament) can now be passed, against the veto of the Lords, after a delay of one year or (if a money Bill) one month.

It must be remembered that most of the functions of the House of Lords raise no controversies at all. Nearly every week during the session there is some debate in that House which arouses more interest than the debates in the House of Commons. The Lower House must spend by far the greater part of its time on Government legislation and on finance. The remainder of the time is devoted usually to matters in party controversy, raised by the Opposition as part of the process of keeping the Government efficient and

106

educating the public in the issues which will be placed before it at the next election. There is neither time nor opportunity to discuss some of the broader issues of policy, such as those which relate to foreign affairs, defence, colonies and Commonwealth relations, which do not require immediate legislation and are not in party controversy. Nor indeed is the House of Commons qualified to discuss these subjects from a detached point of view. It is a group of active politicians representing the point of view of ordinary people. Some of the peers, on the other hand—usually the peers of the first generation, the life peers and the bishops—have a broader experience which on the one hand prevents them from being efficient politicians and on the other hand enables them to make useful contributions on special topics. In this respect the House of Lords is complementary to the House of Commons, and the fact that there is apt to be a preponderance on the Conservative side is immaterial because the debate does not put the Government in peril and rarely even produces much criticism.

In the second place, the peers undertake a mass of work on Government legislation which must be done somewhere. No Government Bill is perfect when it reaches the House of Commons, because neither the civil servants concerned nor parliamentary counsel have had time to study the subject exhaustively. Suggestions for improvement keep pouring in so long as the Bill is in Parliament, and indeed long after. Even if the Bill were perfect when it reached the House of Commons its perfection would be sullied by the time it reached the House of Lords, and a 'cleaning up' process would be necessary. In the House of Commons, too, the Minister in charge may have undertaken to 'consider' all kinds of bright ideas which were new to him, and this 'consideration' by officials on his behalf may produce amendments in the House of Lords. All this requires or may require a somewhat lengthy committee stage in the House of Lords. Sometimes there are as many as 20 pages of amendments moved and accepted. Blue blood is not an essential qualification for this kind of function; possibly a committee appoined by the General Council of the Bar would do it better; it could be done in the House of Commons itself if there was no Second Chamber; but it must be done somewhere if our statute book is not to be an even stranger document than it is now.

In the third place, the House of Lords undertakes a considerable volume of committee work which receives no publicity but which very considerably relieves the House of Commons. It relates to private Bills, provisional orders, special orders, statutory instruments, etc. If these functions were not undertaken by the House of Lords they would probably not be undertaken by the House of Commons. It must be remembered that the latter House consists mainly of active politicians who like to hear themselves talk and to feel the limelight playing on them. Some of them are 'part-time politicians' who drop in for an hour or two in the evening after office hours. There are perhaps two or three hundred members who are prepared to undertake the humdrum tasks of no political importance which bring no publicity; but they are already heavily burdened. Even now it is difficult to find members willing to sit on committees and even more difficult to persuade members sitting on committees to read the necessary documents. So long as there is a House of Lords some of this work is taken by the peers; and if it were not the complaint of 'bureaucracy' would be even more vocal.

It was formerly the view of the Labour party that the House of Lords should be abolished and not merely reformed: and a proposal to that end was inserted in the party manifesto of 1935. There has been no such proposal since, and it seems that opinion has changed. Naturally, the Labour party could not accept the view of the Conservative party—not always put forward blatantly but implicit in the argument— that a Second Chamber is needed to stop radical or 'revolutionary' measures; and indeed the use of such arguments leads opponents to suggest the radical or 'revolutionary' measure of abolishing the House of Lords. When the problem is taken out of this emotional context, however, it is usually agreed that there are functions which a Second Chamber can perform and which could not be performed so well by a Single Chamber system of government.

Unfortunately, this sort of problem is usually discussed in an emotional context. It is too difficult to raise when there is no 'politics' in it and too difficult to settle when there is. In 1909–11 it was discussed in the context of Mr Lloyd George's budget and Home Rule: in 1917–18, when the Bryce Committee considered it, Home Rule was still in issue; in 1947–48 the nationalisation of the iron and steel industry was in the background. Nevertheless, over the past fifty years there has been a gradual approach towards agreement. It has therefore proved possible to introduce minor reforms of some importance. In 1958 the Queen was empowered to create life peers (including peeresses), who are entitled to receive writs of summons and to sit and vote in the House of Lords. The object was not merely to enable persons to accept peerages without saddling the heirs male of their bodies with titles which might prove incongruous. It was also to strengthen the authority of the House of Lords by adding to it persons eminent in different walks of life who could contribute to its proceedings. It was not unwelcome to the Labour party because it would enable a Labour Prime Minister to keep the House of Lords going without advising the Queen to create more hereditary peerages. Indeed, it was hoped in some quarters that, after an interval, the creation of new hereditary peerages would cease. Unfortunately, the life peerages have to be baronies, and there is a convention that Cabinet ministers who are prepared to serve in 'another place' should have earldoms or viscouncies. In any case, the Conservative Prime Ministers from 1958 to 1964 did not diminish the number of hereditary peerages created; they merely increased the number of peers by advising the creation of life peerages also.

The Life Peerages Act of 1958 also created an anomaly. The number of hereditary peeresses is small because most peerages created by letters patent have been limited to the person designated and the heirs male of his body, and so could not descend to females. There were, however, a few cases of special remainder, and also a few 'baronies by writ', deemed to have been created in letters patent in the very early parliaments and to descend to heirs general; and the heir might be a woman. Because of the decision in Viscountess Rhondda's case in 1922, however, no peeress could sit and vote. The Life Peerages Act, on the other hand, allowed women to receive life peerages and to sit and vote in the House of Lords.

This anomaly was removed by the Peerage Act of 1963. That Act also increased the number of hereditary peers by allowing Scottish peers to sit and vote. In accordance with the Act of Union, Scottish peers met in Edinburgh, whenever a new Parliament was summoned, to elect sixteen of their number to sit in that Parliament. Now, they all sit. The main purpose of the Act was, however, to enable a person who succeeds to a peerage to disclaim it within twelve months of succeeding, or within twelve months of coming of age, without affecting the rights of his successors. In consequence of an amendment made in the House of Lords, designed to enable Viscount Stansgate (Mr Wedgwood Benn) to disclaim, a person who had already succeeded to a peerage before the commencement of the Act could disclaim within twelve months after the commencement of the Act. It was this provision which enabled the Earl of Home (Sir Alec Douglas Home) and Viscount Hailsham (Mr Hogg) to disclaim their peerages and be elected to the House of Commons.

The effect of this legislation of 1958 and 1963 is mixed. The power to disclaim applies only to persons who succeed to peerages, not to persons upon whom peerages are conferred. Accordingly, it does not much weaken the House of Lords; and the fact that two Conservative Cabinet Ministers disclaimed under the transitional provision is purely fortuitous because it arose out of the resignation of Mr Macmillan from the office of Prime Minister. On the other hand the creation of life peers (who cannot disclaim) has strengthened the House. At the same time the addition of some thirty Scottish peers and twenty hereditary peeresses to the normal membership of the House has increased the problem of the 'backwoodsmen'. The House of Lords now has over a thousand members, most of whom attend rarely or not at all. Those who do attend are now entitled to first class railway fare and to an expense allowance of up to $4\frac{1}{2}$ guineas a day. An attempt has also been made to persuade 'backwoodsmen' to take leave of absence, though only a minority have done so. Clearly the simplest solution is to separate the right to a writ of summons from a hereditary peerage, so that a peer would have a writ of summons for life if he had once received a writ of summons, but not otherwise. This would gradually reduce the number of Lords of Parliament until, after a generation, the House would consist of the archbishops, the bishops, the hereditary peers who had received writs of summons, and the life peers. If it was also agreed that a Prime Minister would not in future advise the creation of hereditary peerages, the number of such peerages would gradually be diminished as peerages became extinct through the failure of male heirs of the body or (in the case of baronies by writ) heirs general. A Second Chamber consisting of Lords of Parliament for life (or, in the case of bishops, for shorter terms of office) may not be ideally composed, but it would continue the excellent traditions of the present House of Lords, followed by the active peers, without the unnecessary inflation due to some seven hundred 'backwoodsmen' who attend only if and when their interest is aroused.

CHAPTER V

THE MONARCHY

The difficulty of explaining the process of government lies in the fact that it depends so much on intangible relationships which are more easily felt than analysed. This is particularly true of the Crown. On the one hand it is easy to exaggerate the influence of the monarchy by adopting a legalistic attitude and emphasising the part played by the Crown in the theory of constitutional law. On the other hand it is easy to minimise the royal functions by stressing the great trilogy of Cabinet, Parliament and People. The truth lies somewhere in between, but it is not a truth easily demonstrated, nor is it constant in its content. So much depends on private interviews which political scientists do not attend, and so much on the personalities of those who do attend.

The Queen has one, and only one, function of primary importance. It is to appoint a Prime Minister. Somewhere in every Constitution founded on responsible government there must be someone who takes the first step to form a new Government when a gap is threatened. Inevitably that function is exercised here by the Queen. Frequently it is almost automatic. When the Labour party secured a majority at the general election of 1964 there could be no doubt that Mr Wilson had to be Prime Minister. If a party secures a majority and that party has a leader, that leader must become Prime Minister. When the Labour party secures a majority, there can never be any doubt, because the party always insists on the right of the Labour members of Parliament to choose their own leader. The Conservative party does not follow this practice. Mr Baldwin became leader in 1923, Mr Chamberlain in 1937, Mr Churchill in 1940, Sir Anthony

Eden in 1955, Mr Macmillan in 1956, and Sir Alec Douglas Home in 1963 because they were Prime Ministers. The formality of election—now by a meeting of Conservative members, peers and candidates—was in each case followed, but it was a mere formality, an expression of confidence in the leader chosen by the monarch. The process by which Sir Alec Douglas-Hume was appointed in 1963 has, however, led to a change of practice, worked out by Sir Alec himself. There is a sort of preliminary election by the Conservative members of Parliament. This will not bind the Queen, though there will be every incentive for her to appoint the person so designated. It has, however, solved the problem of securing a Conservative leader of the Opposition. Mr Heath was designated by such an election in 1965, and was then formally elected by the Conservative peers, members and candidates.

The Queen thus has a choice when the Conservative party has a majority but no leader, or when no party has a majority. In the former case, her duty is to appoint a Prime Minister who will command the willing support of the party majority. When a Prime Minister retires, it may be assumed that he will advise as to his successor. It is true that Queen Victoria did not ask Gladstone's advice in 1894. She had already decided to send for Lord Rosebery. It would have been better if she had asked because she would at least have heard of the difficulties involved in appointing this 'dark horse in a loose box'. Nor is it certain that Edward VII asked Lord Salisbury's advice in 1902, though Balfour's accession was so obvious that advice was hardly necessary. Again in 1908 it appears that Edward VII did not consult Campbell-Bannerman; but Asquith had been presiding over the Cabinet during the Prime Minister's illness. No information is available as to the appointment of Mr Chamberlain in 1937, but it is a reasonable presumption that Mr Baldwin had been consulted. In 1940 the Labour party insisted on Mr Churchill as the price of its joining a Coalition. In 1963 Mr Macmillan advised the appointment of the Earl of Home (who disclaimed his peerage and became Sir Alec Douglas Home because he was a Knight of the Thistle). There was, however, a not very seemly struggle to push forward leaders for some weeks before Mr Macmillan made up his mind; and the Conservative party has since adopted a new procedure for electing its leader, though this would not limit the Queen's prerogative.

These examples show how frequently a successor is clearly indicated by the political situation. In Lord Rosebery's case, the succession was almost inevitable. In some cases, however, there is no inevitability. A problem arose on the resignation of Bonar Law in 1923. Lord Curzon was the only minister with long experience, because most of the Coalition Unionists had resigned with Mr Lloyd George in 1922, Mr Baldwin was the obvious candidate from the House of Commons, but his Cabinet experience was limited to the eight months of the Bonar Law Government, and until the Conservative revolt of October 1922 he had been at most a quite obscure junior minister. Apart from the defects of Lord Curzon's character immortalised in the lines—

> I am George Nathaniel Curzon,
> A very superior person,

he was a peer. Lord Rosebery and Lord Salisbury had led governments from the House of Lords; but, in the first place, these precedents were not happy, especially Lord Rosebery's; and, in the second place, the position was now different because the Labour party was the official Opposition and was practically unrepresented in the House of Lords. George V thus had a very difficult problem to solve. After consulting several Conservative statesmen, he decided, rightly as is generally thought, to summon Mr Baldwin. Again, on the resignation of Sir Anthony Eden in 1957 it was not clear whether Mr R. A. Butler or Mr Macmillan would be the more suitable Prime Minister. After consulting elder statesmen, the Queen chose the latter.

115

The function is equally important where no party has a majority or the position is otherwise complicated. Thus, on the resignation of Mr Baldwin's Government on its defeat in the House of Commons, after a general election, in 1924, George V was called upon to decide whether to summon Mr Asquith, as leader of the Liberal party, or Mr Ramsay MacDonald, as leader of the Labour party, or some other person who might, perhaps, try to form a coalition. He decided to send for Mr MacDonald, who in fact had behind him only about one-third of the members of the House. The events of 1931 were even more complicated. The Labour Government, which had no majority, had resigned, and the country was passing through what was called a financial crisis. A general election was out of the question and the Labour party was the largest party in the House. The King commissioned Mr MacDonald to form a coalition and was much criticised for doing so; but there is no evidence that he acted unconstitutionally. The action of Mr MacDonald, on the other hand, is not easy to defend. He not only remained in office when he and his colleagues had collectively decided to resign: he also committed the deadly sin of splitting his party and keeping it out of office until Mr Churchill became Prime Minister in 1940.

Such examples do not occur very frequently, but they show the importance of the function. The monarch is in a favourable position because he is in close contact with the Government, though he rarely has opportunity for studying Opposition leaders, particularly where, as with the Labour party in 1964, they have been out of office for a long period. At the same time he is, or ought to be, impartial. Even monarchs have their prejudices, as Queen Victoria showed: but at least they are less partisan than active politicians.

In many other cases the Queen exercises functions, but for the most part they are formal. She is present at Privy Council meetings when the more important kinds of delegated legislation are passed. She appoints Ministers, ambassadors, judges,

116

The Lords mutilate the Ballot Bill, 1872

military and air force officers, senior civil servants, and so on. She summons and dissolves Parliament. She creates peers and confers honours. She assents to legislation. In nearly every case she acts on the 'advice' of Ministers; that is, the effective decision is that of the Cabinet, the Prime Minister or the Departmental Minister concerned. Where a formal act is required she is obviously in a position to ask for explanations and to give advice. The Privy Council is a purely formal body and no discussion takes place. If, however, a Draft Order in Council is brought up, the Minister concerned usually attends. Either before or after the meeting, therefore, the Queen can ask for an explanation.

Even where no formal act is required, however, the Queen can ask for explanations and give advice. She receives a copy of the Cabinet 'minutes' and also of the 'daily print' of telegrams circulated by the Foreign Office. She follows debates in Parliament by means of the *Official Report*. These supplement the information which she receives from newspapers, from personal inspections, and from interviews. Moreover, she has a staff to keep her informed of the developments of political life. For these reasons, if she chooses to devote herself to the study of affairs she can acquire a considerable knowledge of British politics. Though personally remote from Parliament and platform, she is constantly close to the scene of great events.

The sovereign's capacity to influence them depends upon his personal qualities. It would be unreasonable to expect that he will be more than an ordinary man. The Hanoverians were not chosen for their intellectual qualities, and in any case no family produces a genius in every generation in the direct line of descent. Neither George V nor George VI could claim more than industry and common sense. These, however, are qualities which, if used at the centre of affairs, can be extremely valuable. Few of our Ministers are more than plain men. The nation could throw up thousands of men as competent as any of the recent Prime Ministers (other than Sir

The Queen opens Parliament

Winston Churchill). In fact, the British people has a suspicion of intellect and imagination, except in war time. The
sovereign, like a Minister, has a part to play in public. Unlike a Minister, however, he is not compelled to maintain a
glib assurance in matters of politics. He has no cause to be
a partisan, and there is no tendency for him to be satisfied
with the slick slogans that sometimes muster as arguments.
The besetting sin of politicians is that they tend to believe
what they say. A little grain of salt in public life is often
salutary. A king like George V and a statesman like Mr
Baldwin could hobnob as equals. A king like George V
could puncture Mr Lloyd George's rhetoric (unless he were
carried away by it, which also is possible) as a pin punctures
a balloon. Mr Gladstone, complained Queen Victoria,
'addresses me as if I were a public meeting'. She was the
most chilling of his audiences, though she succumbed, as no
public meeting ever did, to Disraeli's blandishments. A
sovereign who can keep his head (metaphorically) can do
immense good, simply by injecting a little common sense.

On occasions, something more is required. The right of
dissolution, for instance, is not solely within the competence
of the Prime Minister. A sovereign who thought that the
power was being put to serious abuse could refuse to allow a
dissolution. The occasion has not recently arisen in this
country, though in 1910 there was some hesitation. In other
countries of the Commonwealth, however, the problem has
at times been acute. If a Prime Minister advised a dissolution
merely because he was no longer in agreement with the
majority of his colleagues—like General Hertzog in 1939—
the sovereign would be fully entitled to refuse. If Mr
Chamberlain had (as he would not in fact have thought of
doing) advised a dissolution in May 1940, when the Germans
were invading Belgium, the King would have been justified
in refusing.

In other words, there are occasions when the 'formal'
functions cease to be merely formal. Normally, the sovereign

would not refuse to grant a peerage to any person recommended by the Prime Minister, though he would be entitled to make representations if the character of the person seemed to make a peerage unfitting. He would not, however, allow 900 or more peers to be created in order to give a majority in the House of Lords unless he felt that public opinion really demanded it. He might thus require, as in 1910, that a general election be held on this specific issue.

The fundamental principle which governs his action in such a case is that his prerogative is not to be used for purely partisan ends. He himself must neither be nor seem to be a partisan. Unionist politicians in 1913 demanded that George V dissolve Parliament without 'advice' from the Liberal Government. The demand was foolish because, though the monarch's co-operation is necessary for a dissolution, ministerial co-operation is equally necessary. It therefore could be regarded only as a demand for the king to dismiss his Ministers on the specious argument that they had no 'mandate' for Home Rule. Had George V acted in this way, he would have shown himself to be a partisan, to be in other words, a Unionist.

It must be emphasised, however, that these problems are exceptional. Far more important than the monarch's governmental functions are what Bagehot called his 'dignified' functions. The process of government is not a question merely of securing loyalty and efficiency in the public services. Vast tracts of government are with us left to unpaid amateurs. Peers, aldermen, councillors, magistrates, members of Royal Commissions and advisory committees, the thousands of persons engaged in voluntary social services and philanthropic societies, give their time and experience to the public weal. Nor is Government just a matter of giving orders and enforcing obedience. It requires the willing collaboration of all sections of the people. Democracy is government by the people as well as for the people. Individuals must feel a personal responsibility for the collective action.

119

To say all this is merely to say that patriotism within limits —the kind of patriotism which is co-operative and not aggressive—is an admirable principle. A people at war cannot fail to be impressed with its importance; but it is equally important in time of peace. It is of course not necessary to have a monarchy to have patriotism. The Fifth Column has been found in monarchies, and the great republics are not deficient in patriotism. Nevertheless, a monarchy provides a useful focus for patriotism, particularly where it has a long and glorious history. If England had remained a republic after 1649, or had become a republic in 1688, it would by now have acquired that aura of sentiment which attaches to *la patrie* or the Constitution of the United States. Until 1760 the Stuarts carried more 'romance' than the Georges.

Nevertheless, the more concrete the symbol the more effective it is. The State functions more easily if it can be personified. An elected President who has stepped out of politics is no substitute for a monarch who has stepped in by right of inheritance. Still less is an active politician, like the President of the United States, a substitute. We can damn the Government and cheer the Queen.

This personification of the State in the monarch requires, to be fully effective, that he be active in good works. Gladstone rightly complained of Queen Victoria's retirement for many years after the death of the Prince Consort. The effect of Disraeli's persuasion was visible at the Jubilee of 1887 and the Diamond Jubilee of 1897. The 'little old lady' caught the popular imagination just when the extension of the franchise required the popular imagination to be stimulated. Perhaps, indeed, it was a little too inflamed. It may be that Milner and Joseph Chamberlain could not have had their war in South Africa if the line between patriotism and jingoism had not been crossed.

This is, however, a matter of opinion. Certain it is that democratic government is not merely a matter of cold reason

120

and prosaic policies. There must be some display of colour, and there is nothing more vivid than royal purple and imperial scarlet. During the present century, therefore, we have placed almost an intolerable burden on the royal family. They must not only head subscription lists and appear on State occasions; they must, also, inspect this and that, open this and that, lay this stone and that, and undertake a thousand other dull tasks in a blaze of publicity.

The medieval 'romance' which surrounds the Queen is not, however, without its disadvantages. Patriotism can easily slop over into jingoism, though there has been very little evidence of it in the present century. Moreover some of the relics of the Victorian age are no longer suited to modern conditions. Queen Victoria established the monarchy on a firm foundation while society was still highly stratified, and quite reasonably only the top strata were associated with the Crown. During the past fifty years, and particularly during the past twenty years, 'Society' in the Victorian sense has almost disappeared, and the effect of maintaining the traditions of the Victorian court has been to associate the Crown with wealth instead of what used to be called 'breeding', with the result that between the wars it was thought of by many as a bastion of that 'capitalist exploitation' which they professed to regard as the characteristic of the economic system. Now that wealth in turn is tending to disappear through heavy direct taxation and death duties, a new technique is gradually being worked out so as to avoid the suggestion, of which the Conservative party has from time to time made use, that the Crown is one of the appendages of that party.

Though the Commonwealth outside the United Kingdom is not within the province of this book, it would be ungracious not to mention the functions which the Crown performs in cementing the various and indeed variegated portions of the Commonwealth. The functions which the Queen performs in person for the independent members of the Commonwealth are few and of no great practical importance; but the problem of creating a common sentiment is even greater in the rest of the Commonwealth than it is in the United Kingdom, and the existence of the Crown helps to solve that problem. There are 600 million people in the Commonwealth each of them concerned primarily with the welfare of his own community. There are over twenty independent nations—with different histories, traditions, languages, economies, interests and cultures. The strange entity called the Commonwealth of Nations is amorphous and, in appearance, almost mystic. It is difficult indeed to recognise in it some central theme which gives it unity and character without overemphasising the part played in it by the United Kingdom. Until recently it was thought that 'allegiance to the Crown', which is itself something of a fiction, might serve as the link. As soon as India became an independent country, however, it became clear that even this fiction must disappear. In the Commonwealth Declaration of 1949 the King was 'recognised' as 'the symbol of the free association' of the independent member nations of the Commonwealth 'and as such the Head of the Commonwealth'. How to make that symbol effective as a symbol is one of the problems which the British Constitution as well as the Commonwealth has to face.

CHAPTER VI

ADMINISTRATION

I. ADMINISTRATIVE BODIES

Parliament and political parties operate for the most part in the light of day. They are, so to speak, constitutional instruments of publicity. The ordinary individual therefore has a substantially accurate notion of the part they play. The delicate balance of relationships and the degree of emphasis to be given to functions are matters for the practical politician and the expert; but the elector is fully entitled to make up his mind on their utility and efficiency. Knowledge of the working of the Cabinet system is less widespread because so much of it is secret. Yet the Cabinet occupies the centre of the stage. It is 'the Government' which is blamed if things go awry and—more rarely—praised if things go well. Its members are in Parliament and are leaders of the parties. Its actions arouse public interest and its functions are well known. The British Constitution would not work, however, if there were not thousands of less publicised persons engaged in the detailed working of the institutions of government.

The complexity of the British system of administration arises partly from history, but above all from the wide range of functions which it has to fulfil. It must be remembered in the first place that in Northern Ireland much of the administration is conducted under the control of the Parliament of Northern Ireland and not under that of the United Kingdom. Consequently, there is an administrative system quite distinct from that of Great Britain. In the second place, the administrative systems of England and Scotland have never been completely assimilated, so that generally speaking the Ministry of Housing and Local Government, the Ministry of

Agriculture, Fisheries and Food, and the Ministry of Education exercise functions in relation to England and Wales only. There are separate Departments in Scotland under the general control of the Secretary of State for Scotland, who also has some functions which in England are exercised by the Home Secretary. There are, further, two distinct sets of local government institutions. Finally, the judicial systems are distinct, with the result that the administrative apparatus which they require is divided, the Lord Chancellor usually exercises functions in England and Wales only, and there are two sets of Law Officers.

It must also be emphasised that it is not easy to determine where 'administration' ends and 'private enterprise' begins. There is, for instance, a group of public utilities—much less numerous since the spate of 'nationalisation' under the Labour Government of 1945–51—such as omnibuses, water undertakings, and the rest. They are regulated under special powers conferred by Parliament, though some are governed by local authorities, some by companies, and some by commissions. In this field 'company' usually indicates private enterprise; but it is not uncommon for Parliament to authorise the formation of a company simply as an instrument of government, while the word 'corporation' (as in British Broadcasting Corporation and British Overseas Airways Corporation) often implies that the organisation is under more or less direct State control. A 'commission', too, may be a body designed to control private enterprise or a body created to operate a nationalised business. We have a National Coal Board, a British Transport Commission, Electricity Authorities, and Gas Councils, all acting as agents of the State. Purely governmental functions are also exercised by other bodies, sometimes mere voluntary associations: examples are the Law Society, the General Medical Council, the Dental Board, the Architects' Registration Council, and the Nurses' Registration Council. It is very difficult to know where to place such bodies as the British Broadcasting Corporation, the Metropolitan Water Board, the Port of London

Authority, Trinity House, river boards, marketing boards, and so on. The explanation is, as usual, that the British Constitution is essentially empirical. An existing body is given a new function, or an old function is transferred to a new body, or a new body is created to exercise a new function, simply as it appears most convenient at the time. The growth in the functions of the State has caused hundreds of new bodies to be created, and has conferred new duties on hundreds of existing bodies. Their methods of organisation, their powers, and the extent to which they exercise them, are known only to those who are specially concerned with each group.

Fortunately, now that they have been mentioned they can be ignored. They certainly create difficult problems, particularly in their relation to other branches of government. From a social or economic angle they cannot be ignored, because many of them have powers of compulsion or of monopoly which closely affect the interests of ordinary people. We shall soon reach the stage where it can seriously be asked whether we have democracy when we are governed by a vast array of boards, commissions, corporations, companies, authorities, councils, and the rest, whose relation to Parliament or to a local electorate is remote. Problems of this order must, however, be discussed either at length or not at all. They are different in respect of each social function.

For our present purpose, also, we can ignore the local authorities. It must certainly be remembered that they exercise some of the most important and the most intimate functions of the State. It has been well said that modern civilisation rests on drains and sewers; and local authorities are not concerned with public health alone, but also with education, police, housing, planning, and the rest. There are problems here, too, but they are much less urgent and no less technical than those relating to other minor bodies. The fact that local authorities are directly responsible to the people solves the major difficulty.

The essential problems of a general order are those relating to the central Departments of State, which function under the control of ministers responsible to Parliament. Here, too, the consequences of increasing State functions are obvious. At the beginning of the eighteenth century the Departments of State were the Lord Chancellor's Department, the Treasury, the Privy Council Office, the Privy Seal Office, the Admiralty, the Offices of the two Secretaries of State, the War Office, and the Post Office. All these remain, though the Admiralty and the War Office have been absorbed into the Ministry of Defence. The Offices of the two Secretaries of State have expanded into the Foreign Office, the Home Office, the Commonwealth Relations Office, the Colonial Office, the Scottish Office, the Welsh Office and the Offices of the Secretaries of State for Defence and for Education and Science. There is also, in Mr Wilson's Government, a First Secretary of State and Minister for Economic Affairs. In addition there are the Board of Trade, the Ministry of Agriculture, Fisheries and Food, the Ministry of Labour, the Ministry of Health, the Ministry of Transport, the Ministry of Social Security, the Ministry of Housing and Local Government, the Ministry of Works, the Ministry of Aviation, the Ministry of Power, and so on.

It is not easy to generalise about these numerous bodies, because it is fallacious to assume that their functions are in all respects equivalent. Their methods of organisation are different because they have to undertake tasks of a very dissimilar character.

The Departments may be classified as follows:

1. Defence

The Royal Navy, the Army, and the Royal Air Force were, until recently, controlled by different Departments, the Admiralty, the War Office and the Air Ministry, though after 1945 they were co-ordinated by the Minister of Defence, who presided over the Defence Committee of the Cabinet and received the advice of the Chiefs of Staff. He alone sat in the Cabinet. The reason for the separation was that different techniques were required for the deployment of the three armed forces and that separate provision had to be made for much of their equipment, such as ships, aircraft, artillery, tanks and landing-craft. The provision of equipment and stores which were common to all the services could be arranged through a network of committees working under the general direction of the Defence Committee and the Minister of Defence. The integration required by modern warfare, however, resulted in a gradual assumption of powers by the Ministry of Defence. In 1964 the three separate Departments became, in effect, sub-departments, with Ministers of State for the Royal Navy, the Army and the Royal Air Force, all under a Secretary of State for Defence.

2. *External Relations*

The Foreign Office is one of the simplest organisations because its functions are to a substantial degree of a 'political' order. Though it has the Diplomatic and the Consular Services under its control, it has not to take such a vast number of technical decisions as most Departments. Its main task is to collect information on which political decisions can be taken by the Foreign Secretary or the Cabinet. The Commonwealth Relations Office similarly is concerned more with policy than with technical decisions. In fact, its lower branches are shared with the Colonial Office. That Office is primarily concerned with the recruitment and promotion of officers in the few remaining colonies and protectorates, and with control over the decisions of colonial governors and other administrators. It may be noted that functions of a similar order are exercised by the Home Office in relation to the Channel Islands and the Isle of Man.

3. Administrative Control

Since many of the functions of the State are exercised by the numerous bodies outside the central administrative system, powers of control are exercised by central Departments. Thus, the Secretary of State for Education and Science has control powers over local education authorities. The Ministry of Transport has powers of control in respect of the highway functions of local authorities, and over the transport undertakings of the British Transport Commission. The Ministry of Power has similar powers over electricity undertakings and over the gas undertakings of Area Boards. The Ministry of Agriculture, Fisheries and Food has control over the agricultural powers of local authorities, over catchment boards and drainage boards, and over the special boards and commissions created in recent years for dealing with various agricultural and fishery problems. The Home Office controls the police, fire brigade, and local election machinery. The Ministry of Housing and Local Government controls most of the other functions of local authorities. In many cases, it will be realised, there is a differentiation in Scotland, where the Scottish Office or a Department under its control takes the place of the appropriate English Department.

4. Direct Services

If we omit the defence services, the oldest service which is provided directly for the benefit of citizens is the Post Office. In recent times, however, there have been notable extensions of these services. The Ministry of Health provides the National Health Service. Since 1966 pensions, social security benefits, and the supplementary payments formerly made by the National Assistance Board have become the responsibility of the Ministry of Social Security. A service which can hardly be described without explanation as for the benefit of citizens is the prisons system, which is operated by the Prison

Commission under the control of the Home Office. The Home Office also has direct control over the Metropolitan Police.

5. Law Enforcement

Law enforcement is primarily the concern of the police, who are employed outside the Metropolitan Police Area by the local police authorities. It sometimes requires, however, much more positive administration, such as frequent inspection. Much of this also is done by local authorities, such as the branches relating to weights and measures and food and drugs. The Home Office is the controlling body. But sometimes a central Department is directly concerned. Factory inspection and the control of explosives and aliens are under the Home Office, though the Ministry of Labour is concerned with the employment of aliens. The Ministry of Agriculture, Fisheries and Food is concerned with plant and animal diseases.

6. Assistance to Private Enterprise

This function cannot easily be differentiated from the others, because it tends to develop into enforcement or control. Thus, the Ministry of Agriculture, Fisheries and Food is primarily concerned with assistance to farmers and fishermen. Demands arose, however, for financial and not merely technical assistance, and financial assistance involves some elements of control. Similarly, the Mines Department was concerned with assistance and enforcement, but the Ministry of Power has powers of control through the National Coal Board. The Board of Trade and the Ministry of Agriculture, Fisheries and Food still assist by the provision of information and in other ways.

129

7. Ancillary Services

The greatest of the ancillary services is the provision of money and the control of all Government expenditure. This is the special function of the Treasury, which raises taxation through the Commissioners of Inland Revenue and of Customs and Excise. Money is also obtained from the Crown Estate Commission and the Post Office. Financial control also means control over Departmental estimates and over contracts. It has led, too, to general control by the Treasury over the Civil Service. Finally, the Ministry of Public Works and Buildings provide the buildings and furniture required by the Government Departments and their numerous outposts.

It must not be thought that the above gives a complete survey of governmental functions. It does, however, illustrate their variety. It is enough to show that many classes of civil servants are required. The Post Office, for instance, employs postmen and men engaged in the carriage of mail, telephone and telegraph operators, engineers, sorters, counter assistants, an immense clerical staff engaged in checking, accounting, docketing and the rest. The naval dockyards, the ordnance factories and the Ministry of Public Works employ skilled, semi-skilled and unskilled workers. Professional men of all kinds—lawyers, accountants, architects, scientists, engineers—are to be found in some or all of the Departments. Every Department requires shorthand typists, typists, cleaners, porters and messengers. Some of the work demands a high degree of skill and knowledge, and is performed by what is known as the 'executive class', while some is almost mechanical. There are special classes such as the factory inspectors, the customs and excise officers, the employment officers in the Employment Exchanges, and the inspectors of taxes. The ultimate decisions are taken by civil servants, under ministerial control, who require the highest intelligence that the nation can produce.

2. THE PROCESS OF ADMINISTRATION

Enough has been said to indicate that it is quite impossible to describe the process of administration. The citizen meets it at many points, the local post office, the telephone exchange, the employment exchange, the office of the inspector of taxes, even, in London, at the street corner. The most important part, however, is that with which he is not directly in contact but which really influences his environment even more because it assists ministers in reaching the decisions which determine the policy of the country. This 'administrative class', as it is called, is very small. It contains only about 3300 people, while Government employees of what are called non-industrial classes number over 600,000 of whom about 250,000 are commonly designated as 'civil servants' by ordinary citizens. These 3300 men and women, however, occupy the key positions in the administrative system. Some of them are so important that their names get into the newspapers in spite of the service practice of anonymity. These are among the most eminent of the administrative class; but that class includes also the young men and women who came straight from the Universities at the latest examinations.

Many of these civil servants of the administrative class are engaged upon what may be called internal administrative tasks. They may be concerned, for instance, with financial relations with the Treasury, or with appointments to and promotions in the civil service. Our primary interest is in policy-making. It will therefore be convenient to assume that the administrative class exercises that function alone. If we take the hierarchical system of a Department like the Ministry of Health, we find that it is somewhat as follows:

The Minister
Private Secretary
Assistant Private Secretary
The Parliamentary Secretary
Private Secretary

131

The Permanent Secretary
Private Secretary
The Deputy Secretary
8 Under-Secretaries
26 Assistant Secretaries
46 Principals
Assistant Principals

The Minister and the Parliamentary Secretary are members of Parliament. In some Departments the Parliamentary Secretary exercises some of the functions which would normally be exercised by the Minister, either because there is a traditional allocation or because the Minister specially delegates certain of his functions. Generally speaking, however, the Parliamentary Secretary's functions are parliamentary; and inside the Department he is concerned partly to advise himself about the many problems which may arise in Parliament and partly to assist generally by commenting on documents and attending or presiding over committee meetings.

The Permanent Secretary is the permanent head of the Department, and his position has been likened to that of a general manager. He exercises general control, he has the last word on proposals that go to the Minister, and the first word on proposals that come from the Minister. The Deputy Secretaries (in some Departments there are two) give general assistance to the Permanent Secretary and perhaps pay special attention to certain aspects of the Department's work.

The Under-Secretaries are concerned with the separate branches of the work of the Ministry. In the Ministry of Health, for instance, one deals with finance, another with the establishments, and so on. Where the work is large, an Under-Secretary might be assisted by Assistant Secretaries. A less heavy section of the work might not require an Under-Secretary at all, but would be in charge of an Assistant Secretary. The Principals give these senior officials, as well as the senior technical officials, general assistance by writing

132

memoranda, commenting on other people's memoranda, acting as secretaries to Departmental Committees, summarising the contents of files, analysing statistics, and so on. The Assistant Principals do the same kind of work, but they are younger and less experienced, and their main task is to learn the process which will fit some of them to become Permanent Secretaries. The Minister will probably have a Principal as private secretary, while the other private secretaries will probably be Assistant Principals.

The function with which we are here concerned is the taking and execution of decisions. Regarded from the angle of the civil service, this involves tasks of three kinds. First, there is the collection and analysis of information. The accumulated wisdom of the Government is to be found not merely in the minds of ministers and civil servants, nor even in the files of memoranda, but in the libraries of books, despatches, reports, and so on. Information on anything within the range of the Department may be required quickly. The Foreign Office provides the best example, because everybody knows that a constant succession of telegrams comes in from British representatives abroad. The Foreign Secretary, the Permanent Under-Secretary,[1] the Deputy Under-Secretary, perhaps even an Assistant Under-Secretary will have an interview with an ambassador or a minister or a counsellor of embassy or legation, and a note is promptly taken for purposes of record. Such foreign representatives may also bring or send documents. Newspapers and press-cuttings provide information which may be more or less accurate than that provided from official sources, but which must be read and checked. Eminent people write books whose contents must be known. Not much of this information may be immediately relevant. Ruritania may be off the map, so far as the Foreign Office is concerned, for a decade. Suddenly, however, news comes that a delicate situation has

---

[1] Where there is a Secretary of State the 'general manager' is called, not Permanent Secretary, but Permanent Under-Secretary of State.

arisen because the Crown Prince has been assassinated, or a general election has brought in an unfriendly Government, or some British subject has been imprisoned. At once everybody from the Prime Minister to an Assistant Secretary clamours for a full but concise account of the whole background. There has to be somebody in the Department who knows something about it and, above all, who knows exactly where in the files of the Department is to be found the material for a complete story.

The provision of information is an ancillary function without which action is likely to be bad because it is, so to speak, performed in the dark. The essential function of the administrative class is in the taking of decisions. In the days when the present Cabinet system was established, it was possible for a minister to take every important decision himself. We find Peel and Gladstone, for instance, corresponding not merely about the principle of tariff reduction, but about points of detail. Sir James Graham at the Admiralty did not personally order the crew of a man-of-war to reef the topsail, but he knew everything that went on in the Admiralty. Lord John Russell and Gladstone drafted clauses in Bills. Every appointment was made in fact and not merely in form by a minister. He required only a principal adviser, a few technical officers and some clerical assistance.

This history is important, because it was under Peel, Russell and Gladstone that the theory of Cabinet Government was established. Yet in 1842 the national expenditure was in the region of fifty million pounds. The civil service, including all classes, could not have contained more than 40,000 people. In 1963–64 the 'ordinary' expenditure was over six thousand million pounds and the civil service numbered over 600,000. A ten-fold increase in the work does not mean that the minister takes ten times as many decisions, particularly when it is remembered that his parliamentary and political functions have also increased and that most of these cannot be delegated. It means that the modern minister takes few of the decisions, though the number varies from the Foreign Office, where so many are 'political', to the Post Office, where the Postmaster-General takes very few.

Many decisions are of course purely matters of routine. When an unemployed insured person 'registers', he is aware that the Minister of Social Security personally knows nothing whatever about him, and that some minor official decides whether he is entitled to benefit. Even where there is a discretion the decision may be taken far down the hierarchy. A local officer of the Ministry of Social Security has power to determine whether certain supplementary allowances are paid to an unemployed person or pensioner. Matters of wider importance, however, go up as far as an Assistant Secretary. A housing scheme, for instance, would ultimately receive the approval of such an official. Similarly, any question of principle would go as far. No person of a lower status than an Assistant Secretary would sign a document on behalf of a minister. Subject to any instructions that might be issued, a problem would be sent higher up only if it was of special difficulty, or was unusual, or might involve political controversy. If several branches of the Department were concerned, several persons would have remarks to make, and in the absence of agreement it might have to be brought before a Departmental Committee (which is not to be confused with a committee of outside persons appointed by the minister to make a report). If two or more Departments were concerned, it might be necessary to have an inter-Departmental Committee.

The great majority of questions are, however, 'departmental questions'. They involve the exercise of a wide and informed discretion. Formally, many of them will go to the minister. If he is wise, he will deal only with those which are indicated to be important. It is the duty of the Permanent Secretary to see that everything of importance is submitted to the minister. It is the minister who is responsible, and he

135

if anybody will be criticised in the House of Commons. On the other hand, it is equally the duty of the Permanent Secretary to see that the minister is not bothered by questions of a minor order. The questions submitted to the minister are, however, more numerous than those which might strictly be called 'political'. Such questions, and such questions only, must ultimately be put before the Cabinet. This is particularly true of proposals involving substantial expenditure or the passing of new legislation, or which concern more than one Department, or which may be discussed in the House of Commons. The minister must be prepared to make positive proposals on these matters, and must therefore make up his own mind: but in addition he will consider questions of a departmental nature, perhaps involving administrative reorganisation, or a change of policy, or the appointment of a committee of investigation.

Thus, there is a hierarchy of decisions which may be classified as follows:

Routine and minor discretion	Executive class
Discretion within a policy	Assistant Secretary
Departmental policy	Permanent Secretary and Minister
Government policy	Cabinet

This is a very rough classification indeed, because the division cannot be expressed in words. The important fact is, however, that a very large number of decisions is taken by senior civil servants. Moreover, even if a decision is taken by the minister or by the Cabinet, the case must be prepared. The information available must be collected by a Principal or an Assistant Principal, who will, at least if he is asked to do so, add his suggestions as to the line to take. His memorandum will be read by an Assistant Secretary, who may send it forward with his comments, or throw it in the waste-paper basket and write another, or hand it over to another and more senior Principal with the request to put the information in a sensible form. Other Assistant Secretaries may have their remarks to make. The file may go to another Department for comment. Under-Secretaries, Deputy Secretaries and Permanent Secretaries may add words of agreement and disagreement. The files which precede the introduction of a great local government reform, for instance, must be extremely bulky. Knotty problems will be discussed by committees. Precisely where in this process the minister comes in depends partly on him and partly on the problem. At the end, however, there lies before him a definite statement of the practicable alternatives, with the arguments for and against each of them. He can see the files if he wishes, but generally there is no need, because the combined wisdom of the Department has brought the question down to an issue where common sense and political *savoir faire* are the qualities required. If he says that he must consult the Cabinet, he makes up his own mind and gets an Assistant Secretary (who perhaps gets a Principal) to state the case in a Cabinet memorandum.

Somewhere and eventually the decision is taken. Then comes the third function, that of execution. The higher the decision goes, the more general it is likely to be, and the greater the need for interpretation. A decision to raise the school-leaving age, for instance, would be taken by the Cabinet. That decision would involve a large number of consequences relating to more schools, more teachers, additional education grants, maintenance grants for scholars, the needs of Church schools, and so on. Some of these questions are so important that they would be considered by a Cabinet committee. Others could be decided in the Department or by discussion with the Treasury. There might be questions about the school medical service to be discussed with the Ministry of Health. Questions relating to the release of scholars in special cases would be raised by or with the Ministry of Labour. In the Department itself somebody would have to consider the less important questions so as to instruct the draftsman. He in turn would raise points which seemed to him to need settlement one way or the other.

There would be discussions with outside persons and bodies —perhaps the Archbishop of Canterbury, the leaders of non-conformity, the Association of Educational Committees, the National Union of Teachers, and so on. Memoranda would be prepared to form the basis of the minister's speeches: amendments would be examined and reasons given for not accepting them. Finally, when the Bill is passed, the administrative machinery must be set in motion. Regulations must be drafted, circulars sent out, forms designed, proposals from education authorities considered, difficulties discussed and overcome. In little of all this would the minister take part. There is the same division of functions according to the importance of the issue.

3. BUREAUCRACY

Accusations of 'bureaucracy' usually relate to minor aspects of the process. It is said, for instance, that too wide powers can be exercised by the issue of Statutory Instruments. It is complained also that differences which ought to be submitted to the courts are settled by 'ministers' (which means 'civil servants'). These are important complaints because they involve the rights and interests of individuals. They have been shown, nevertheless, often to be based on a misconception of modern administrative law. The State exercises new and wider functions which require quite a different technique of government from that suited to nineteenth-century conditions. The destruction of *laissez-faire* does not imply destruction of the methods used for the administration of private and criminal law, because the old functions remain and nothing suggests that the methods used for their execution were fundamentally wrong. These methods are not appropriate, however, for social insurance, planning, housing, and other twentieth-century functions.

The general problem caused by the growth of State functions is more important. In part it has been met by an increase in the number of Departments, and therefore of ministers; but this raises increased difficulties of co-ordination which are discussed in Chapter VII. In part it has been met by the creation of subordinate Departments. Experiments in this direction have not proceeded far, and apparently they were not considered so successful that the number of cases had to be increased. The first effort was made in February 1916, when the Parliamentary Under-Secretary of State for Foreign Affairs was promoted to the Cabinet as Minister of Blockade. He remained subject to the general control of the Foreign Secretary, because the blockade involved questions of foreign policy, but he was free to take day-to-day decisions within the ambit of the Foreign Office policy. Also, by securing liaison with the Admiralty he was able to remove the many causes of friction which had developed between the two Departments in 1915.

The Ministry disappeared at the end of the war, but in the meantime the Department of Overseas Trade had been set up at the end of 1917. The reason for its establishment was the conflict of opinion between the Foreign Office and the Board of Trade as to who should control the commercial services, overseas-trade commissioners in the British Empire, commercial attachés in British legations, and consuls. Eventually it was decided to put the trade commissioners and the attachés under a new joint Department, though the consuls remained under the Commercial Department of the Foreign Office. The joint Department had at its head a Parliamentary Secretary, who was responsible both to the Foreign Secretary and to the President of the Board of Trade. As Under-Secretary of State for Foreign Affairs he also controlled, subject to the Foreign Secretary, the Commercial Department of the Foreign Office. It survived until the war of 1939, when it disappeared.

The third Department, the Mines Department of the Board of Trade, was set up under a Parliamentary Secretary in 1920. The then President of the Board of Trade stated that the Parliamentary Secretary 'should be in a position of complete responsibility so far as all the routine work of the Department is concerned, and should only be responsible to the President of the Board of Trade in matters which really involve large policy'. The proposal was criticised on the ground that ministerial responsibility would be 'frittered away'. 'With that kind of divided responsibility', said Sir Leslie Scott, 'the British Constitution will never work.' During the next twenty years, nevertheless, the British Constitution did not break down, and the Department remained in being until it was incorporated into a separate Ministry of Fuel and Power. The system does not destroy ministerial responsibility, it makes it more effective; for the alternative is to allow decisions of substantial importance to be taken by civil servants. Far from being reprehensible, it provides a precedent which might be followed. It enables decisions of importance to be taken by ministers without increasing the number of separate Departments and thus aggravating the problems of co-ordination.

During the war of 1939–45, when administration inevitably became heavy, Mr Churchill discovered a new method which has been followed by subsequent Prime Ministers. This was to allocate 'Ministers of State' to overworked Departments. A Minister of State can be allocated responsibility for part of the work of the Department so that the officials can submit papers to him. In the great majority of cases he will be able to decide on his own responsibility, but if the problem is difficult he will act only after consulting the Minister, for the Minister remains responsible to Parliament. In the Conservative Government of 1959 there were four such Ministers. In the Labour Government of 1966 there were fourteen. They are considered to be of Cabinet rank and therefore have more authority than Parliamentary Secretaries, though they are not in fact in the Cabinet. Quite often the Minister of State deputises for the Secretary of State when the latter is engaged on other duties. For instance, the Minister of State for

Commonwealth Affairs may be discussing matters with the Government of Malta, while the Secretary of State is discussing matters with the Government of Kenya. When the Kenya Ministers go back to Africa, the Secretary of State may take over the problems of Malta.

Another device is used in the Ministry of Defence, which has not only a Secretary of State but also three Ministers of Cabinet rank, called Ministers of Defence for the Royal Navy, the Army and the Royal Air Force.

However numerous be the Ministers, and however the political strength of the Government be deployed, most decisions must be taken by civil servants or, in the Ministry of Defence, service officers. There is, nevertheless, one very real check which prevents delegation to civil servants from giving rise to bureaucracy. The responsibility of ministers to Parliament means that every decision, even if it is taken far down in the official hierarchy, may be criticised in Parliament. If a member considers that injustice has been done to an individual, or a wrong principle is being applied, he may ask the minister privately for an explanation. If he is not satisfied, or if he chooses not to use this method, he can ask a question in the House. If the answer does not meet his criticism, or if he thinks the subject important enough in any case, he may raise the subject in debate. By these means decisions are brought to the personal attention of ministers and, if they think that the criticisms have any value, they necessarily insist on Departmental investigation. Let us take a few examples at random. On a particular day in 1940, the Secretary for Mines was asked about short-time in the pits of Lancashire, the Minister of Shipping about dry-dock accommodation at Newport, the Postmaster-General about licences for wireless sets in military camps, the Minister of Health about a pension for Mr C. F. Mott, and so on. It is possible that none of these matters had received ministerial attention before the questions were put down. Even if a minister gives a soothing answer, if there is any real difficulty there is a Departmental investigation.

Even more important than the fact that questions are asked is the fact that questions may be asked. The minister is compelled to deal with any matter which may be raised in Parliament. A civil servant is compelled to remember that his minister may get into a parliamentary wasps' nest if a decision proves to be unacceptable. The result may be, not that the minister decides too little, but that he decides too much. Ministers must not make mistakes; therefore civil servants must not make mistakes. Consequently, it is complained that as compared with private enterprise a service like the Post Office is characterised by timidity. It tends to follow a routine, and where decisions have to be taken such care is shown and such caution exhibited that the whole question becomes wrapped in yards of 'red tape'. Many of those who make this accusation often make the accusation of what appears to be the opposite defect, that decisions are taken by 'anonymous whipper-snappers' instead of by ministers. There is, of course, some truth in both complaints. It is inevitable that decisions should be taken by civil servants; it is also inevitable that some of them should tend to pass on their responsibility to their superiors, or to give such careful attention to a problem that a decision always comes too late.

There is no real harm in decisions being taken by civil servants. On the contrary, it is a waste of a minister's time to insist on his attention to a problem that raises no political issues. At the same time, it must be remembered that the line between political and administrative decisions is very fine. Moreover, even when the minister takes the decision or puts it before the Cabinet, the civil servants express their own views. It is not to be expected, nor is it to be desired, that officials of this calibre should not. The result is, however, that there is a 'Departmental policy' independent of the minister and the Cabinet. It bows to political decisions, but it has profound effect on them. A minister who has no strong views of his own is almost certain to adopt the

Departmental policy. A minister who has views of his own finds that, with the best will in the world, civil servants discover hosts of objections to his proposals when they conflict with their own ideas.

This 'Departmental policy' must not be regarded as something formalised. It is not to be found expressed anywhere. It is certainly not a bureaucratic conspiracy. It is simply the product of the collective experience of the senior civil servants and of the bent of their minds. It has been possible to speak of 'Treasury orthodoxy' in matters of finance. Indeed, we often hear references to the 'Treasury mind'. The Foreign Office was alleged to have francophil tendencies during the period when many people were profoundly suspicious of French foreign policy. The Colonial Office was formerly accused of Arab sympathies in relation to Palestine. It was asserted that the India Office was more sympathetic to Muslims than to Hindus, not for the reason given by the Congress politicians, that Great Britain desired to divide and rule, but because British administrators in India found Muslim culture more attractive than Hindu culture. It is not necessary to suggest that these assertions were true. They could never be proved because the evidence is necessarily too scanty. It is enough to point out that they could be made. It is assumed, in other words, that there is a Departmental policy which persists in spite of changing ministers and changing Governments.

Its importance must not be over-emphasised. No principle is more firmly fixed or more consistently carried out than the fundamental principle that ministers determine policy. When the Government decided in 1932 to turn its back on free trade, the Treasury officials at once put their minds to devising the best possible tariff system. Mr Arthur Henderson, who was not accustomed to maintain amiable fictions for the sake of politeness, has borne witness to the spirit in which the Foreign Office assisted the change which he made in British foreign policy. Nobody can complain that the civil service did not labour manfully to make a success of the socialist schemes of the Labour Government of 1945–51. After thirteen years of Conservative Government, the civil servants of 1964 with remarkable celerity adapted the machinery of government to suit Mr Wilson's opinions.

The system is nevertheless full of difficulties. Senior civil servants are able men, often more able than the ministers whose orders they take. Their arguments necessarily carry great weight. They would be failing in their duty if they did not frankly point out the difficulties which they foresee. Simple solutions attract politicians who do not see the ramifications of the consequences. It is the business of a Department to prevent a minister from making mistakes. Nevertheless, even the most expert may be wrong. No doubt it is possible now to give a verdict on the policy of 'appeasement' which Mr Chamberlain and Lord Halifax carried in 1938. It was not so easy to do so in 1938. Assuming that the Foreign Office was against appeasement, it is not easy to say precisely how emphatically they should have pointed out its dangers. Moreover, it is not merely a question of reaching a decision. Palmerston showed that, even when a policy has been adopted, it can be ruined by failure to put it into execution enthusiastically. To decide upon appeasement is not enough. Every step taken in foreign policy must be determined by that principle. If those who have the day-to-day responsibility of drafting telegrams believe that it is fallacious, they will necessarily act hesitatingly. It is certain that they would not try to sabotage a policy, as Palmerston did deliberately in 1851; but they would occasionally seek to minimise what appear to them to be the probable and undesirable consequences.

The allegation that in 1937 Sir Robert Vansittart was 'kicked upstairs' to the newly created office of Diplomatic Adviser and superseded as Permanent Under-Secretary of State because he agreed with Mr Eden and disagreed with Mr Chamberlain may not be true—he took a large part in the execution of the policy of appeasement as a member of the Foreign Policy Committee which was mis-named the Inner Cabinet. The fact that it could be plausibly maintained shows the existence of the belief that there may be occasions on which Departmental policy runs so emphatically counter to ministerial policy that a change of officials is necessary if the supremacy of ministerial policy is to be maintained. Similarly, it was alleged that that very able administrator Sir Evelyn Murray was transferred to the Board of Customs and Excise in 1934 because the views which he had formed during twenty years' service as Secretary to the Post Office were an obstacle to the reforms which Sir Kingsley Wood had decided to carry out.

How often problems of this kind arise it is impossible to say. They are capable of arising without reference to changes of Government. They might arise with even greater effect where policy was suddenly changed through a change of Government. Let us suppose that after the Entente Cordiale had been established in 1903 with the enthusiastic support of the Foreign Office, the new Liberal ministers had decided in 1905 that the policy was fundamentally wrong. Could we expect the same enthusiasm from the Foreign Office in carrying out the opposite? The position might be even more acute where a Labour Government succeeded a Conservative Government. The views which Sir Richard Hopkins of the Treasury laid before the Royal Commission on Unemployment Insurance in 1931 were emphatically condemned by many Labour politicians. The opinions which Sir Maurice Hankey stated to the Royal Commission on Armaments in 1935 ran directly counter to the Labour party policy. These were examples of the few occasions on which civil service opinion becomes known. It is obvious, however, that some senior civil servants might be profoundly distrustful of Labour party policy. Not all of them have personal experience or even knowledge of the segments of society which give the Labour party its ethos. It is reasonable to assume that the Treasury has none of the suspicions of the Bank of England exhibited at Labour party conferences. The Board of Trade can hardly be unsympathetic to the eminent industrialists and leaders of commerce who from time to time give it assistance.

On the other hand, there was no difficulty when the Labour Government of 1945 took office. So far as is known, no senior official was removed to another post or 'kicked upstairs' because he could not work with his Labour Minister or help to carry out a Labour policy. There were a few unexpected appointments, but there is no evidence that they were due to political opinions. Had there been political bias in appointments the Conservative Opposition would not have hesitated to say so: for when Labour supporters were appointed to the new public corporations Conservative members did not hesitate to shout 'Jobs for the Boys'. Though the internal stresses and strains of the civil service are very properly never disclosed in public, it seemed to outside observers that the civil service had adapted itself remarkably well to a new political system.

It is no doubt true that the absence of a fundamental division between the parties made the process easier. The national insurance scheme was a development of a system which was begun by the Liberals and carried on by the Conservatives. The national health scheme was new and more revolutionary, but it was the kind of scheme which, on a smaller scale, the civil service had been accustomed to handle. The nationalisation schemes were, in the main, developments from various controls and methods of assistance produced by previous governments, while the public corporation system had been exploited on previous occasions. It is also true that the war provided a period of transition. From a Chamberlain Government to an Attlee Government would have been a startling change. The principal Labour Ministers had, however, been in office since 1940, except for the short period of Mr Churchill's 'Caretaker' Government in 1945. Mr Attlee was Deputy Prime Minister, fought an election, and became Prime Minister.

There was more change in 1964, but it consisted mainly of a reshuffling of the official staff to suit the changes in the machinery of government which Mr Wilson wished to bring into operation forthwith. Also, several experts of known Labour sympathies were brought into the administration to assist the Labour ministers in the detailed formulation of the policy which had been expressed in general terms in the Labour party's election manifesto. None of them, so far as is known, had taken part in electioneering. They were brought in as experts, not in order to provide 'jobs for the boys'. The idea was evidently suggested to Mr Wilson by President Kennedy's use of a 'brains trust' from the American universities. The experts were given leave of absence by their employers, usually universities or colleges of universities. There is, nevertheless, danger in the idea that there are Conservative experts and Labour experts. It seems to assume that civil servants cannot be trusted to advise on policy because they are not sufficiently biased. What is more, the intrusion of politics into the public service is the first step towards the 'spoils' system and eventually towards corruption. Britain has avoided these problems, and it has done so by insisting on three principles which are aspects of the same principle. The first is that the Minister is responsible, morally as well as technically, for every action of his Department and must resign if it is seriously at fault. The second is that parliamentary criticism of a civil servant is fundamentally unconstitutional and objectionable. The third in that the civil servant should be politically impartial and give the best advice that he can whatever be the policy or programme of the Government.

CHAPTER VII

CABINET GOVERNMENT

I. MINISTERIAL RESPONSIBILITY

The peculiar contribution of the British Constitution to political science is not so much representative government, which is an obvious solution, as responsible government. Added to representative government, it means that government is carried on by persons who are responsible to the representative House of the legislature, the House of Commons. Responsibility is secured by placing control of administration in the hands of politicians who are either members of or are represented by political subordinates in the House of Commons. So long as there is a House of Lords and ministers are unable to speak in both Houses, it is necessary that a few ministers should be in that House. It is not a very desirable arrangement, since neither the approval nor the disapproval of the House of Lords has much effect on Government policy, and the political issues are fought out in the House of Commons. Though it is not desirable that a person should be disqualified for ministerial office because he is a peer, he has considerable difficulty in exercising his main function through a subordinate minister in the House of Commons. Naturally, the peers like to have a few senior ministers in their own House, but the essential political task is in the House of Commons. If the Foreign Secretary is a peer, as Lord Home was in 1961, the House of Commons is deprived of authoritative expositions of foreign policy, because another Minister is a mere representative, and an overworked Prime Minister cannot be familiar with all aspects of policy. Moreover the effective criticisms

148

of that policy are made in the House of Commons, where the parliamentary opposition is to be found, and it is necessary that the minister should be familiar with the atmosphere in which criticism is made and that he should be on the spot to defend himself. On the other hand, to authorise ministers to speak in both Houses would be to place a substantially increased burden on their shoulders. That burden is already so great that it should not be increased. The real solution is to insist that all the heads of the great Departments should be in the House of Commons, though it would require as a corollary that peers should be capable of election to the House of Commons and that there should be an adequate number of Ministers of State in the House of Lords. In Mr Wilson's Cabinet of 1966 there were only two peers, the Lord Chancellor and the Lord Privy Seal. Four of the Ministers not in the Cabinet, namely two Ministers of State at the Foreign Office, a Minister without Portfolio and the Minister of Defence (R.A.F.), were peers.

The responsibility of ministers to the House of Commons is no fiction, though it is not so simple as it sounds. All decisions of any consequence are taken by ministers, either as such or as members of the Cabinet. All decisions taken by civil servants are taken on behalf of ministers and under their control. If the minister chooses, as in the large Departments inevitably he must, to leave decisions to civil servants, then he must take the political consequences of any defect of administration, any injustice to an individual, or any policy disapproved by the House of Commons. He cannot defend himself by blaming the civil servant. If the civil servant could be criticised, he would require the means for defending himself. If the minister could blame the civil servant, then the civil servant would require the power to blame the minister. In other words, the civil servant would become a politician. The fundamental principle of our system of administration is, however, that the civil service should be impartial and, as far as may be possible, anonymous.

A political rally in Trafalgar Square

Complication arises from the fact that all decisions of considerable political importance are taken not by ministers as such but by the Cabinet. In normal times, the Cabinet contains all the heads of the more important Departments. The minister at the head of a Department is, so to speak, the representative of the Cabinet in relation to matters within the jurisdiction of his Department. Consequently, it is never very clear whether the minister is speaking as head of the Department or as the spokesman of the Cabinet. The House is not informed of the distribution of responsibility between the minister and the Cabinet. Often the question is one which in practice is decided by the House of Commons itself. The importance of a question is in large degree a parliamentary matter. If unemployment benefit is refused to John Smith of Rotherham, it is reasonably certain that the Minister of National Insurance knows nothing about it. If, however, the honourable member for Rotherham takes up the matter, it is at once raised to ministerial rank and the minister has to look into the matter. If the whole Opposition takes up the question because it appears to be a gross example of ministerial neglect or political discrimination, then it is almost certain that the Cabinet will have to discuss the matter.

The Cabinet is said to be collectively responsible for the whole policy of the Government, whether it has been brought before the Cabinet or not. This principle assumes that defective administration by or under the control of any minister should be laid to the door not of the minister but of the Cabinet. In practice, however, the principle is never carried so far, because it rests with the Cabinet whether they shall accept or disown the ministerial decision. If the Cabinet chooses to disown the decision, then the minister alone will resign. If the Cabinet chooses to accept the decision as its own (as appears to have happened when Sir William Joynson-Hicks in 1928 announced the intention to make the franchise for women the same as that for men), the

Cabinet will treat the matter as one of confidence in itself. This choice is open even if the decision criticised was that of the Cabinet itself. For instance, the Hoare–Laval agreement of 1935 apparently had Cabinet sanction; but so great was the popular reaction that the Baldwin Cabinet (which was unusually timid before public opinion) decided to repudiate it. Sir Samuel Hoare was therefore allowed to make himself a scapegoat and to resign his office of Foreign Secretary.

If a decision is supported by the Cabinet, the question becomes one of confidence in the Government. The whips are put on, and members must take the responsibility either of supporting the Government or of risking their resignation or a dissolution of Parliament. In practice, for reasons already given, the party majority supports the Government. No majority Government in recent years has had serious cause to fear a parliamentary defeat. Accordingly, the decision of the Cabinet to support a minister is really based not on possible parliamentary consequences, but on the effect which the decision may have on public opinion. With very rare exceptions, all questions in the House of Commons are matters of confidence; and what really matters is not the support of the House but the support of the people. Once again, therefore, we find that vocal public opinion provides the fundamental test.

Ministerial responsibility to the House of Commons is thus the means of assuring that government is in tune with popular opinion. A responsible government cannot be a bureaucracy; and it is for that reason that emphasis is laid so strongly on the principle that for the decision of a civil servant some minister must be responsible. It is true that there have been many recent examples of bureaucratic instruments deliberately established in order to avoid ministerial responsibility. The public corporations set up under the legislation of the Labour Government of 1945–51, for instance, were deliberately given a large amount of independence. They were made subject only to 'general directions' from their appropriate Ministers, who refused to answer detailed questions in Parliament even where they had the power to ask for information. They considered that nationalised industries should be as independent of political control as competitive industries, so far as day-to-day administration was concerned, and that only general policy should be under ministerial and therefore parliamentary control. The National Assistance Board provides another example established for a different reasons. It was thought that the discretion of granting National Assistance allowances should be completely divorced from political control. The principles upon which discretion was exercised, as set out in the Regulations, should receive the approval of Parliament (though Parliament should have power only to accept or to reject, not to amend). It was also thought that the amount of money to be made available to the Board should be under parliamentary control. But it was desired that the administration of discretion in individual cases should be freed from political influences.

This second example exhibits a suspicion of Parliament which has never been justified. It may have been true that when the 'means test' was imposed by local authorities the principles upon which they operated depended on their political opinions. There is no evidence, however, that they discriminated among recipients according to their politics. Still more certain is it that Parliament could not be an instrument of political discrimination among individuals. That a Labour majority would favour higher rates and a more generous discretion than a Conservative majority is obvious; but there is nothing in the position of the National Assistance Board which prevents the House from determining general policy. It must always be remembered that the decisions of the House are the decisions of the Government. The Government whips are put on, and the majority votes with the Government. If there were individual discrimination, therefore, the Government would be responsible; but nothing is more certain than that any Government which attempted to discriminate in this way would lose heavily at the next general election. There is no 'corruption' in the wide sense in which that term is used in North America, because the electorate has been educated for a century in 'clean politics'. Any Opposition would be delighted to receive a single example that it could put on every hoarding and repeat in every election speech. In fact, therefore, the National Assistance Board has been a complete failure as an 'independent' institution. It is neither more nor less subject to political control than the Ministry of National Insurance would be, and the only result of its 'independence' has been to create a fruitful source of inter-Departmental conflict. If anything went wrong, the officials of the National Assistance Board would blame the officials of the Ministry of National Insurance, and the officials of the Ministry would blame the officials of the Board.[1]

It is also necessary to emphasise that ministerial responsibility means only that a politician must be able to answer in the House of Commons for every act of administration. Emphasis is necessary because 'ministerial responsibility' has become a slogan which is regarded as being a reason in itself, and the reason behind it has been forgotten. When, for instance, proposals have been made for vesting minor decisions in Parliamentary Secretaries, or for vesting major decisions in 'Super-Ministers', the opponents have at once brought out the slogan. The fact that the Secretary for Mines, before the creation of the Ministry of Fuel and Power, used to answer for matters within his Department instead of the President of the Board of Trade did not infringe ministerial responsibility. On the contrary, it made it more effective: for, if there were no Mines Department, there would be a Mines sub-Department. In other words, decisions taken by a junior minister would be taken not by the President of the

---

[1] The National Assistance Board ended in 1966 when its work was taken over by the newly created Ministry of Social Security.

Board of Trade but by the Under-Secretary at the head of the sub-Department. The House would be able to question the President of the Board of Trade, but the effective decision would be taken by a civil servant. The result of creating the Mines Department was that Parliament could criticise a minister who in all probability had himself taken the decision. Similarly, the existence of a Minister of Defence does not detract from ministerial responsibility but increases its efficacy. Instead of asking three separate ministers to answer for the major problems of defence, the House can ask the Minister, who has had them under consideration. The effect of placing major responsibility in the Minister of Defence has been, in addition, to enable the three ministers in charge of the Defence Forces to control administration in more detail. They can answer more questions on the basis of their own knowledge. Ministerial responsibility does not mean undivided responsibility—it is always shared at least between the minister and the Cabinet; it means only political responsibility. The more ministerial responsibility is divided by adding to the number of ministers, the more effective the responsibility; though, of course, every new division adds to the problem of co-ordination.

2. THE CABINET

The Cabinet can always have the last word. In peace time most of the items on its agenda are brought up from the Departments. In the normal process of government, problems of a political order are met, new projects are considered, perhaps new legislation is required. Every Department concerned with the social and economic life of the country has in its pigeon-holes projects for reform which it is anxious to carry through when money and parliamentary time can be found. Even when there is no 'cold war', questions of foreign policy have to be considered. Somewhere within the far-flung borders of the Commonwealth there are problems requiring immediate solution. No change or development of policy of any importance would be carried out without Cabinet sanction. If it required much money, the Treasury would certainly require prior Cabinet approval. If legislation were needed, the Cabinet must certainly decide upon it. In any other case the minister concerned would consider whether he could take the responsibility alone; and if he were in doubt he would consult the Prime Minister.

The Cabinet is also the court of appeal where two or more Departments differ about matters which affect them both or all of them. Administration does not fall neatly into thirty sections, in such a way that no dispute can exist as to the bounds of Departmental activity. Indeed, nearly every important problem cuts across Departmental boundaries. Even if no other Department is affected, the Treasury is almost certainly interested. On purely inter-Departmental matters, the Departments would try to reach agreement. If they found themselves unable to agree, the Prime Minister might act as arbitrator and co-ordinator. In the last resort there must be appeal to the Cabinet. In fact, however, many inter-Departmental questions are of a Cabinet order in any case.

Nor is there anything to prevent a minister from raising a question which does not affect his Department. The examples cannot be frequent, but they can be found. Joseph Chamberlain had opinions about most things. He did not think that his functions as President of the Board of Trade prevented him from discussing Home Rule with Parnell. Nor did he think that, as Colonial Secretary, he had nothing to do with social reform. Any minister may have views about foreign policy. Above all, the Prime Minister exercises a general oversight of the policy of the Government. He can no longer follow Peel's example and keep in touch with the work of every Department, but at least he must watch that ministers do not go joy-riding with Departmental policy.

Questions of this nature are, however, usually thrust upon the Cabinet by the logic of the political system. They are to be found in the party programme at the last election; or they are raised in the House of Commons; or they arise because some foreign power, or some section of opinion at home or in the Commonwealth, takes action which makes them urgent. Once a week foreign affairs are the first item on the agenda, Foreign Office telegrams are circulated daily, and, if some urgent question is raised, it is inevitable that the Cabinet should deal with it. Moreover the House of Commons can raise any matter to Cabinet rank by making enough fuss about it. The Cabinet may prefer to let sleeping peers lie, but if a few members of the other House insist on debating the reform of the House of Lords, the Cabinet must decide either to do something or to do nothing. The Colonial Office may be entirely satisfied with its African policy, but the Opposition can keep the question on the Cabinet agenda. Here once more we meet that close relation between government and public opinion which needs to be stressed so often. Public opinion can rouse Parliament and Parliament can rouse the Cabinet. The Prime Minister determines the Cabinet agenda, but in large measure external forces determine what the Prime Minister shall place on it. Moreover the Cabinet's primary concern is to keep itself in office, and its decisions must therefore keep pace with opinion.

In normal times the Cabinet meets for two hours twice a week during the session, and less frequently out of session. This is not much more often than in the reign of Queen Anne. It is able to get through its business for several reasons. In accordance with the general tendency, more decisions are taken in the Departments, and the Cabinet dislikes having referred to it questions which are not of the first order. There is, too, better organisation of its work. Since the full Cabinet was restored in 1919 it has had a Secretariat, which produces an agenda under the Prime Minister's control and circulates documents where the Departments do not undertake to do so. The Cabinet usually insists on having a proposal documented, so that it can be considered beforehand and so that conclusions on it can be reached quickly. Moreover, it insists that no question shall be presented to it until it has been fully discussed between the Departments concerned. In other words, inter-Departmental discussions are conducted between the Departments or the ministers concerned, and do not take the form of cross-talk in the Cabinet unless it is impossible to reach agreement outside the Cabinet. The status of the Prime Minister, also, has so far advanced that, in consultation with the ministers, he can reach decisions which are not sufficiently important to be brought before the Cabinet. Finally, the Cabinet makes constant use of committees, both to reach substantially agreed proposals and to see that a decision reached in principle by the Cabinet is carried out in detail by the Departments.

The pressure upon ministers arises not from long and complex discussions in Cabinet, but from the numerous Departmental questions which they have to settle, from the burden of numerous committee meetings, from the increased demands of Parliament and of the party organisations, and above all from the variety and importance (rather than the number) of the decisions which have to be taken in Cabinet. By the time that a question reaches the Cabinet it has been reduced to first principles. The documents circulated are neither long nor numerous, particularly if we omit the Foreign Office telegrams, which are circulated for information and not for decision. Nevertheless, to decide such questions as those relating to the status of Berlin, the control of inflation, the organisation of transport, the defence of Malaysia, constitutional developments in Africa, a contributory pensions scheme, and the rest, is no easy matter. A statesman's life is not a happy one. He has to determine issues of the most profound political and social significance on what must inevitably appear to him to be inadequate information. Necessarily he must rely upon the Departmental ministers and the Prime Minister. They, in turn, must lean heavily on their advisers. It is not work but worry that ages Cabinet ministers.

The nature of this task gives some indication of the qualities which ministers should possess. Obviously they must be of wide general understanding, capable of seizing quickly the essential points of a problem, and able to give a rapid decision. These qualities are essential for effective decisions, whether in the Department or in the Cabinet. They are included in that elusive but well-understood quality known as 'judgment'. Not all ministers possess it, and often it is the least prominent ministers who do, with the result that there are always members of the Cabinet whose presence is deemed essential by successive Prime Ministers, but whose qualities are rarely understood in the House of Commons. Among the most prominent ministers who appear to have had it during the past sixty years are Balfour, Campbell-Bannerman, Haldane, Baldwin, and Attlee. It must be repeated, however, that sometimes it is possessed by the least prominent.

At least as important is such a knowledge of human nature as enables a minister to choose and rely on able assistants, whether ministers or civil servants. Judgment of this kind does not necessarily go with judgment in the realm of events. Of the statesmen mentioned above only Balfour and Attlee possessed both in any marked degree. Joseph Chamberlain and Lloyd George possessed judgment of men but were deficient in judgment of events. The quality of judging events, in fact, often goes with lack of initiative and imagination. This is not necessarily a defect. In a Prime Minister in peace time it is probably an advantage. In ordinary administration, when no serious problems have to be faced, the good administrator requires sound common sense rather than a fertile imagination. An imaginative minister is probably a volatile minister, like Lloyd George and the two Churchills. Gladstone was not exactly volatile, but he went too fast for his colleagues and his public—though not even 1886 and the last gasp of 1893 can deprive him of his pre-eminence. Peel, the model Prime Minister, had no imagination. Joseph Chamberlain had not much imagination, but he had restless energy which caused more difficulty than all his qualities could offset. Disraeli's imagination fortunately spent itself in dreams, except in foreign and imperial policy, where it produced little wars and might have produced a big one. In war time, on the other hand, imagination and initiative are necessary. At such times the Salisburys, the Asquiths and the Neville Chamberlains ought to be retired, unless they deliver the effective conduct of the war to the Disraelis, Joseph Chamberlains, Lloyd Georges and Winston Churchills.

'Judgment' usually makes a person a good committee man, and this is an essential quality. Yet persuasive committee men are sometimes deficient in judgment. Birkenhead was a little unstable, but an extremely good committee man. Kitchener was not only a bad administrator but a worse member of a committee, because he could neither make his own case nor answer the case put by another. Balfour, on the other hand, was extremely good.

Finally, it must be remembered that ministers are not only administrators but also politicians. They must be convincing in the House of Commons and persuasive in the country. These two qualities generally go together: yet sometimes they are distinct. Gladstone was extremely good both in Parliament and on the platform, but Disraeli was more at home in the House. Joseph Chamberlain was, in a very different way, an able debater and a good platform speaker. Some Labour politicians, however, fail in the House of Commons because their good platform technique is quite unsuited to the House. Ramsay MacDonald was, until about 1929, a political orator of the first class, but he was not effective in the House. The atmosphere is different, interruptions are more frequent, and they require answers, not appeals to the gallery. Peel, who was no orator, was very effective in the House, as even Disraeli admits. In these days, too, we must not forget the

159

influence of broadcasting and television. Great efforts have to be made to convert party leaders into 'television personalities', for they can lose votes by their mannerisms.

The position of a Prime Minister is, however, peculiar, and it is considered more particularly hereafter. The question which we must now ask is whether the nation obtains the ministers that it requires. The primary consideration is that, except for a few peers, they are all drawn from the majority in the House of Commons. The quality of the ministers thus depends on the quality of the majority. Difficulties in this respect have already been mentioned. The standard of intelligence and ability in the House of Commons is higher than it is in the country generally, but it is not as high as it is in the administrative class of the civil service or in the top ranks of the professions or even—though this is more doubtful—among the ablest business men. The prizes of political ambition—power and prestige—are great, and they attract some of the ablest in the country; but it is always true that, outside a handful of members who 'choose themselves' as ministers, almost any member would do equally well and equally badly.

Moreover the choice rests with the Prime Minister. It is, of course, his business to choose a Cabinet which will work as a team, and to choose junior ministers who can work with their political superiors. Randolph Churchills, Harcourts and Joseph Chamberlains usually have to be appointed; but they, and others of the same kind though less able, can be a serious nuisance to the unity and efficiency of a Cabinet. Where it is politically possible, such misfits have to be avoided. A weak Prime Minister, or a Prime Minister with little appreciation of human qualities, may nevertheless mistake criticism for obtrusive ambition or lack of team-spirit. Ramsay MacDonald was both weak and ignorant of men, and his efforts at team-making were extremely poor. They would have been worse if there had not been so many Labour members whose standing in the party compelled appointment. Where no such obstruction exists, such a Prime Minister is apt to choose colourless 'yes-men'. The path to political preferment most often passes through the field of party orthodoxy.

This situation is the more dangerous because, normally, ministers reach the Cabinet through junior offices. It is desirable that it should be so, because the House of Commons is generally a good judge of a minister, and one who does well as Parliamentary Secretary can usually be relied on to make a good Cabinet minister. If, however, junior ministers are members who have always voted straight, who have never opened their mouths except to bleat adulation, and whose title to promotion is that they have politely and unobtrusively carried messages as parliamentary private secretaries for some years, the more able but less compromising members never secure the training which will fit them for the Cabinet. The difficulty must not be exaggerated. The casual reader of newspapers need not be surprised that he knows the names of some private members and has never heard of half the Parliamentary Secretaries. The publicity-monger and the charlatan, the loud-mouthed and the gentle-man of one idea, may secure a reputation outside Parliament when they have none in the Chamber. They supply 'news' because they are obstreperous; and they are frequently obstreperous because they get their names in the papers. Nevertheless, there are in every Cabinet some ministers who surprise everybody except themselves that they have climbed so high. It is not that they are bad ministers, but only that they are very, very ordinary.

Nor must it be forgotten that Prime Ministers are no longer assiduous parliamentary listeners. They have far too much to do, and the Gladstonian tradition that a Prime Minister ought always to be in the House has gradually disappeared. In some degree the Prime Minister must rely on the whips, and the whips like members who speak when they are spoken to and vote when they are told. In other respects, he is apt to know of those who have famous names or have connections in Society. Austen Chamberlain did not get his first step up because of his qualities, substantial though they proved to be, but because he was the son of Joseph; and there have been more flagrant examples.

The problem is not so acute as it might be, because the standard of the majority is usually high enough to produce a few leaders and a general competence among the other ministers. A Joseph Chamberlain thrusts himself into office, but the choice of A rather than of B usually makes very little difference. Moreover, it has been said already that the House is usually a good judge of a minister. Mere cleverness does not succeed, nor does mere oratory. What brought Gladstone to the front was not his roaring torrent of words, but his obvious grasp of the problems of trade and finance. Not all the social prestige nor all the arts of publicity can persuade the House that an eminent nincompoop knows his business. A Prime Minister is bound to choose the really able, and grumbling in the lobbies and criticism in the House prevents him from backing all his private fancies.

3. THE PRIME MINISTER

The Prime Minister holds the key position in the British Constitution, and nearly all recent developments have tended to increase his authority. The extension of the franchise, added to the prestige which Gladstone and Disraeli conferred upon the office, have given him a status almost comparable with that of the President of the United States. A general election is in reality the election of a Prime Minister. The elector has a choice between Gladstone and Disraeli, Salisbury and Rosebery, Balfour and Campbell-Bannerman, Asquith and Balfour, Baldwin and MacDonald, Churchill and Attlee, Home and Wilson. A party which has not a leader is in a hopeless position, and party with a weak leader in a weak position. Indeed, in the Conservative party the leader is the party, for he controls the party organisation and is in command of its funds.

The support which he thus obtains is a party support, but it is a party support concentrated in the leader. The parliamentary majority is a party majority, but it owes allegiance to the leader, and it is spoken of as his majority. It is common to refer to his position in the Cabinet as *primus inter pares*; but this description is now far from being true. He chooses the ministers and determines which of them shall be in the Cabinet. It is true that certain of his prominent supporters choose themselves, but often he is in a position to ignore some of them. Mr Chamberlain could keep out Mr Churchill and Mr Amery, though Mr MacDonald could not keep out Mr Henderson. If he thinks fit, he can ask a minister to resign. He can shuffle his pack as he pleases. He alone determines whether and when Parliament shall be dissolved. It is difficult to turn him out. The party majority must hold together, because if it does not it will probably put the Opposition into power. Some ministers may resign; but they are unlikely to desire to split the majority, and they can do no more than give more or less friendly advice, and more or less detached criticism, from below the gangway. A party which has a leader must usually bear with him; and if the Conservative party is in office, it is the Queen and not the party that chooses the leader.

It is true that the Prime Minister cannot exercise that oversight over Departmental business which Peel exercised. The functions of government are too vast. Nevertheless, he has a special responsibility for the whole policy of the Government. Though the Labour party has consistently criticised the growing power of the office, it has done more than any to increase it. When in Opposition it has consistently concentrated its attack on the Prime Minister, with the result that Conservative Prime Ministers tend to think that they are more important than they are. It is always possible to find a successor.

The office is necessarily what the holder chooses to make it and what the other ministers allow him to make of it. His powers are large, but he has to secure the collaboration of his colleagues. Neither Salisbury nor Balfour could (even if they had so desired) have prevented the limelight from falling on Joseph Chamberlain. On the other hand, not even he could take the centre of the stage while Gladstone was behind the footlights. Rosebery's Government descended to futility because the Prime Minister was not strong enough to control Harcourt. Campbell-Bannerman, on the other hand, increased his strength in the long years of desolate opposition until he became capable of managing even the strong team that took office in 1905. Baldwin allowed his Ministers to stray while Attlee kept them under his thumb. Churchill and Macmillan regarded them all as expendable.

The office really requires varied and quite inconsistent qualities. On the one hand, the Prime Minister as party leader must have a strong personality, capable of dominating the political scene and inspiring confidence in a suspicious electorate. The issue before the country while Gladstone was alive, even when he was not leader of the Liberal party (as in 1880), was not whether there should be a Liberal Government, but whether he should be Prime Minister. None of his successors, except Churchill in 1945, has occupied such a position, though Lloyd George approached it in 1918. On the other hand, what is wanted in the Cabinet is not a dominating personality but a good chairman. Gladstone was not a good chairman because he tended to be the whole committee. He always had a policy of his own, and therefore tended to concentrate on some aspects of government instead of supervising the whole. Churchill, too, had bright ideas on which he liked to make speeches, even in the Cabinet. In wartime he could properly concentrate on war, and the Cabinet gave the grand old man his head; but it is not so easy to concentrate on peace, and whatever merits the Conservative Government of 1951–55 possessed did not depend

164

on the Prime Minister. Indeed, a Prime Minister in peace time ought not to have a policy. If he has able ministers, he ought to rely on them, and policies should come from Departmental ministers, assisted as they are by all the knowledge and experience that their Departments can offer. The qualities which made Lloyd George a great Prime Minister in war time made him a disastrous Prime Minister in peace time, when Curzon at the Foreign Office was 'almost an Under-Secretary'. Salisbury would have been a better Prime Minister if he had not also been Foreign Secretary—and perhaps there would have been no Boer War. Some think that in 1945 the electorate showed remarkable judgment in cheering Mr Churchill as a great war-time leader and at the same time turning him out of office. Attlee was a better peace time Prime Minister because he knew that his job was to persuade his unruly team to reach agreed decisions and stick to them.

The best chairmen have in fact been those who had the least popular appeal. Sir Austen Chamberlain—who served under the five Prime Ministers from Balfour to MacDonald—once told the present writer that the best of them was Balfour, and there is other evidence to the same effect. Balfour's reputation has suffered because he had a difficult task even while Joseph Chamberlain was in the Cabinet pressing tariff reform; it became impossible after Chamberlain was let loose in 1903. Moreover, he was Prime Minister of a Government which had snatched a huge majority out of the apparent end of the Boer War. Even if the tariff reformers had not assisted its decline and fall, it would certainly have been heavily defeated in 1905. What Sir Austen Chamberlain meant was that Balfour was superb at keeping a discussion to questions of principle and drawing a conclusion out of it. The difference between Balfour and Gladstone was the difference between a driver who keeps his team going hard even when they want to bite each other, and a driver who lets his team loose and pulls the carriage himself.

Nor are the Prime Minister's conciliating and encouraging

165

functions limited to the Cabinet. A minister needs an experienced political adviser whom he can consult. Balfour was prepared to listen, consider, and advise. Baldwin was prepared to listen, but generally let the minister decide for himself. MacDonald was not prepared to listen and was incapable of advising. Lloyd George wanted to do all the talking. Moreover, if the Prime Minister is to keep control and to exercise properly his Cabinet function of leading the discussion to a conclusion, he must not only be ready for consultation, he must also take the initiative. MacDonald realised the need for informing himself, but he had a dislike of most of his colleagues, and he was hardly on speaking terms with some of them. He tried, therefore, to compensate by reading endless documents. As a chairman he was fully informed, but there was not that confidence between Prime Minister and colleagues which makes for effective decisions. It may be, however, that all peace time Prime Ministers suffer from the loneliness of the job. They still speak of their political 'friends'; but their Right Honourable friends are really not their friends but their subordinates, and nearly all the subordinates are concerned about their political careers. Though Jones may have political judgment and Robinson lack the elements of common sense, we must not consult Jones and ignore Robinson: but when Robinson advises he expects his advice to be taken. On the whole it is better to be reserved and detached, and therefore impartial; but then one has to 'wander lonely as a cloud that floats on high o'er vales and hills'.

The position is quite different in war time because then one aspect of policy (though it has many facets) dominates the whole political scene. A Prime Minister with a policy, or capable of forming one by consultation, is therefore desirable. He thus requires a forceful personality, capable of securing rapid and effective action. He ceases to be a mere chairman or co-ordinator and becomes chief of a vast war machine. He is, in other words, no longer chairman of the board of directors of a holding company, but managing director of an even larger operating company. It is therefore obvious that the qualities required are quite different. Pitt was not great success even in the conduct of what, in the eighteenth century, was called 'war'. Peel would probably have been a failure because, though a great administrator, he took years to assimilate a new idea. Gladstone would have been a great war minister and Disraeli even a greater, provided that he had had subordinates who paid attention to detail. Campbell-Bannerman and Balfour would have been quite ineffective, while Joseph Chamberlain would have been excellent. Asquith was poor, even before his son's death, while Lloyd George was a success and Churchill, in most respects, magnificent.

4. CO-ORDINATION

Peel's Cabinet of 1841 contained fourteen ministers; but of these, five had no serious Departmental duties. Outside the Cabinet were five ministerial heads of Departments; but of these only the Chief Secretary for Ireland, the Postmaster-General and (perhaps) the Chief Commissioner of Land Revenue, had real Departmental duties. Thus, the Prime Minister and the Cabinet had to co-ordinate the activities of at most twelve Departments. Moreover, each of these Departments had much less work to do than is now the case. It has also to be remembered that, while the Government had Ireland on its hands, in other respects the range of its interests was smaller. There were no United Nations and few nationalist States; though there were colonies there was no Commonwealth. Also, the Army was governed from the Horse Guards, and the functions of the Secretary at War, who was in the Cabinet, were primarily financial. Complete control over the Army was not taken until 1895. Above all, there were no social services except the poor law. Since Departmental work was much smaller, ministers could decide a high proportion of Departmental questions; and since the functions of government were fewer, the Cabinet could decide every problem of any importance.

The size of the Cabinet gradually increased until, in the nineteen-thirties, it contained 22 or 23 members. Since this was too large for effective administration, especially in war time, Churchill kept down the size of his war Cabinets by the device of 'Ministers of Cabinet rank', outside the Cabinet, who were sworn of the Privy Council and paid as Cabinet Ministers, but were called into Cabinet meetings only when matters affecting their Departments were considered. This device was followed by Churchill's successors who kept the Cabinet down to 17 or 18 persons. Wilson in 1964, while keeping seven Departmental Ministers out of the Cabinet, restored the Cabinet to 23 persons. No doubt there were sound political reasons. For thirteen long years—a longer period than any party had had to suffer since the Reform Act of 1832—the Labour party had fought gallantly and stubbornly in Opposition. It was necessary to bring in some new men, but it was also necessary to reward some of the old soldiers.

Each Prime Minister alters the arrangements slightly, partly to suit the emphasis of his party's policy, and partly to suit the personnel at his disposal. There are, however, some 30 Departments under direct Ministerial control, of which one, the Treasury, has two Ministers in the Cabinet, the Prime Minister and the Chancellor of the Exchequer as well as at least one Minister of Cabinet rank but outside the Cabinet. There are, however, many semi-autonomous bodies, like the Board of Inland Revenue, the Development Commission and the Colonial Development Corporation, for whose work a Minister is responsible to the extent of his powers.

The functions of government do not fall nicely and conveniently into thirty sections. The actions of one Department may require the collaboration of several more. It is easy to find examples. The landing of troops in Norway

168

and the withdrawal from Dunkirk in 1940 required the intimate collaboration of the Admiralty, the War Office and the Air Ministry. It required also money from the Treasury, ships from the Ministry of Shipping, transport within Great Britain from the Ministry of Transport, equipment from the Ministry of Supply, and food from the Ministry of Food. Such collaboration is needed, also, not only at the moment of decision and afterwards, but long before. Nobody had, before the war, contemplated that British troops might be landed in Norway; but in the preparation for the event of war it was necessary to assume that an expeditionary force might have to be landed somewhere under the eyes of the enemy, and to make skeleton plans accordingly.

Another example may be drawn from the post-war housing problems. The primary responsibility rested with the Ministry of Health (now the Ministry of Housing and Local Government), but many other Departments were concerned. The site of a housing estate was the concern of the Ministry of Town and Country Planning and access to it of the Ministry of Transport. The supply of labour depended on the policy of the Ministry of Labour and the supply of materials on that of the Ministry of Supply. In certain cases, at least, building would be undertaken by the Ministry of Works, but the responsibility for gas and electricity would rest on the Ministry of Fuel and Power. If after all this the estate was completed, the Ministry of Education would require a school, the Postmaster-General a post office, the Ministry of Food a food office and the Ministry of Labour an employment exchange. Above all, the Treasury would have to find the money. If to these we add the local authorities, the Area Gas Board, the Electricity Authority, the National Assistance Board and all the other authorities concerned, the problem of co-ordination becomes obvious. When it was suggested that there might be a Ministry of Housing it was replied that it would be the fifth wheel of the coach; actually it would be the extra leg of the centipede.

Co-ordination is one of those magic phrases which are apt to be on everyone's lips but which few care to take the trouble to define. For instance, in a debate on economic co-ordination in 1940, the Government's critics were considering different aspects of the problem. Mr Chamberlain thought that he was answering them when he pointed out that they were asking for different things, though in fact he was merely demonstrating that co-ordination was lacking on several different levels of administration. Co-ordination machinery is designed to fulfil several different functions and, though they are closely connected, it is wise to take them separately.

1. Overlapping of Powers

Theoretically, each Department should be doing different things. Two Departments ought not to be in a position to give contradictory orders, nor should it be necessary for an individual outside to approach two Ministries to obtain permission to do a certain act. In practice, it is very difficult to separate powers precisely. For instance, the Ministry of Housing and Local Government is concerned with planning; but planning involves the planning of roads, and the Ministry of Transport is concerned with roads. Again, the Ministry of Agriculture is concerned with common land; but if the common land is a playground it is the concern of the Ministry of Education; and if it is trust property it is the concern of the Charity Commission.

There is far more involved in these examples than a question of overlapping of powers, but they show how necessary it is to define the powers closely in the first instance. Theoretically, this particular problem is not difficult. In peace time powers are conferred by legislation which is approved by the Cabinet. The Cabinet is thus expected to prevent overlapping. In war time, however, the powers are taken by delegated legislation—by hundreds of Orders in Council between 1939 and 1945. Possibly they all went to the

Cabinet, but it is extremely unlikely that they were all read by any single person whose function it was to see that powers were precise and accurate.

2. Encroachment

Even if powers appear to be distinct and without over-lapping, they must be expressed in general language. They are interpreted, however, by the Departments themselves. 'Under legal provision XYZ,' a Department may say, 'we have power to stop so-and-so from doing this sort of thing.' It is possible, however, that 'so-and-so' has already approached another Department and has received per-mission to do what he wants to do, under, say, legal provision ABC. It may be that the two provisions are quite distinct in their terms but are capable of being interpreted so as to give one Department power to prevent and another Department power to permit. It is easy to conceive of confusion in this respect between the powers over wheat production formerly possessed by the Ministry of Agriculture and the powers over flour milling possessed by the Ministry of Food.

If he thought fit, 'so-and-so' could challenge before the courts the validity of the former Department's refusal; but no one likes litigating against a Government Department, and indeed only a wealthy corporation with much at stake would run the risk of being taken from the High Court to the Court of Appeal, and perhaps to the House of Lords. In any case, these august bodies may not have completed their deliberations before the need had disappeared.

3. Duplication

The example given in the previous paragraphs might have been a perfectly proper exercise of quite distinct powers. The one Department might have given permission because, so far as it was concerned, there was no objection; the other might have refused because, so far as it was concerned, there

171

was objection. The reason would be that the problem had to be considered in two aspects, and 'so-and-so' ought to have applied to both. For instance, if Jones wishes to build a house by the side of a main road, he might have to apply for permission to both the county council and the district council. If both refused, he would need to appeal both to the Ministry of Transport and to the Ministry of Housing and Local Government. The former might allow the appeal because, from the angle of road safety, there was no objection; the latter might reject the appeal because the building would be unsightly or would interrupt the view, or would demand unnecessary extension of water mains and sewers. 'Ribbon development' is not a problem of road safety alone; it is, in addition, a problem of uneconomic local services. It is, therefore, the concern of two Ministries.

Examples of inevitable duplication of this kind are numerous. For instance, the Department of Education is concerned with the health of school children because empty stomachs mean empty heads and bad eyes or bad teeth mean bad education. School children are, however, part of the ordinary population whose health is the concern of the Ministry of Health. Moreover, the children may suffer from malnutrition because of the chronic unemployment of their fathers and the consequent dependence of the family on the supplementary allowances paid by the Ministry of Social Security.

The point here is, however, that two Departments may be concerned with an application from the same person to do a single act because that act has two aspects. It would be much simpler, cheaper and more expeditious if he could make one application and leave the two Departments to settle the question in respect of both of its aspects. For instance, it is unnecessary for an application for ribbon development to be considered by two inspectors at different sittings, involving two arguments by lawyers, two sets of costs, two payments for the hire of rooms, and so on.

This kind of duplication is obvious to persons outside the Government service, but there may be other examples not so obvious. For instance, the Foreign Office requires information about public opinion overseas. During the war for this purpose it had representatives overseas who telegraphed summaries of newspaper opinion. It had also an organisation based on the Royal Institute of International Affairs (Chatham House), which summarised newspaper opinion. The prevention of overlapping was an internal question for the Foreign Office. The Ministry of Information, however, must have had information about public opinion in neutral countries if its operations were to be successfully conducted. It would be wasteful to have one 'Chatham House' for the Foreign Office and another for the Ministry of Information.

4. Competition

The Departments are large purchasers of commodities. Except where the commodities are requisitioned, they compete in the open market. This may mean that they compete with each other. For instance, the Army, the Navy, the Air Force, the Post Office, the Ministry of Works, the Ministry of Transport, and many more, all require motor vehicles. The three Defence Services require machine guns, ammunition, food, fuel, huts, and so on. It would be wasteful and ridiculous for Government Departments to bid against each other. Moreover, it is not only a question of preventing competition. If, for instance, the Royal Marines and the Army used different kinds of rifles, costs would be put up because manufacturers would have to follow different designs for the provision of the rifles themselves and all their parts, and also for the provision of ammunition. Stocks available for the one would not be available for the other.

Again, there may be competition for man-power as well as competition for commodities. Not only might there be competition among the Defence Services, but also a competition between the Services and other Departments. One of the weakest points of the organisation in 1914–18 was that the Army was using for the front line, or for fatigue duties, skilled men who were urgently required at home.

5. The Application of Inconsistent Principles

'Policy' is usually said to be a matter for the Cabinet. It has already been pointed out, however, that there is a policy at each level of administration. The Cabinet decides policy in very general terms. For instance, the Cabinet may decide that two new frigates shall be built, at a cost estimated by the Treasury and the Ministry of Defence in consultation at £20,000,000. If the Treasury and the Ministry had agreed on a cost of £19,500,000 or £20,500,000, however, the Cabinet would have agreed as readily. The difference of £500,000 is not a Cabinet question unless the two Departments disagree. There is, nevertheless, a policy involved in the £500,000, which is regarded by the Cabinet as an inter-Departmental matter so long as the Departments are agreed. Having obtained Cabinet sanction for £20,000,000, the Ministry proceeds to elaborate plans (though in fact the outline will be clear already because it was necessary to make a rough plan in order to estimate the cost). If the Ministry decides to build one costing £10,500,000 and another costing £9,500,000, it is unlikely that the Treasury will raise objections: this is a purely Departmental question. Further, the armament to be provided is the concern of the Admiralty Board; but within the lines which they decide the Fourth Sea Lord would have wide discretion. Moreover, though the Fourth Sea Lord would approve the terms of the contracts, there is plenty of scope for discretion by his junior officers.

The fact is that wherever there is a discretion there may be a policy. If there is not, there ought to be, because decisions ought not to be taken except in terms of some consistent principle. Discretionary powers are exercised at least as far down in the civil service as the Assistant Secretaries and frequently much further. Where different Departments are dealing with cognate subjects, however, the principles applied in the exercise of discretionary powers are quite likely to conflict. This is especially clear in economic matters, since a nation's economy is a unit and, indeed, is merely part of world economy. The details of a commercial agreement with Spain, for instance, will be the concern of officials in the Treasury, the Board of Trade, the Ministry of Agriculture, the Ministry of Transport, and perhaps the Foreign Office.

6. Major Policy

The major principles of policy are determined by the Cabinet. Here, it would seem, there is co-ordination and no need to discuss the point further. It is, however, just at this fundamentally important stage that co-ordination used to be weakest. The need for co-ordination of the kind illustrated above has been realised, whereas even Cabinet ministers have failed to realise that often it was in their own activity that the system was weakest. Careful examination of Mr Chamberlain's speech on economic co-ordination in 1940 reveals that he was thinking in terms of inter-Departmental disputes. He gave a long account of the many devices used to settle these problems. He did not meet the criticism of the Opposition because they were thinking in terms of major policy. His view of co-ordination was arbitration between Departments; their view of co-ordination was the formulation of economic policies which needed execution by several Departments. The criticism was summarised in the statement of *The Economist*[1] that 'the Government have no apparent policy on prices, wages, labour mobilisation, exports or finance'; or, in other words, each Department was left to decide without an overriding Cabinet policy.

Proposals on major policy come to the Cabinet from two

[1] Vol. 138, p. 133.

sources. First, they may be brought up by Cabinet ministers themselves and be derived, so to speak, from the ministers' own heads. Ministers are both busy administrators and active politicians, more skilled in taking sensible decisions about other people's ideas than in developing ideas of their own. Nevertheless, many ideas come in through ministers' heads even if they do not originate there. Criticism in the press, and still more often in Parliament, is accompanied by suggestions, often futile but occasionally fruitful, as to the policy to be pursued. Some of the most fruitful ideas start in discussions in technical journals or in journals of opinion, where they are read by civil servants, by members of Parliament looking for material for speeches, by other journalists looking for material to write about, or even by Cabinet ministers. This last process is slow, but, if an idea is a good one, usually effective, because a 'public opinion' is created.

In fact, however, not many ideas become policies by this route. It is a long and exhausting journey, as the history of any great policy—like franchise reform, the repeal of the Corn Laws, Home Rule, or even the United Nations—shows. More often, the policy comes from a Department. It may, of course, have started outside the Department. Civil servants are busy people, but they keep themselves informed not merely from official documents but also from books and periodicals. Accordingly, when a problem has to be solved the solution may be compounded of ideas coming from many sources, both official and unofficial. Before 1940, when the departmental hierarchy was rigid, the problem would start a file which went up and down in the Department until the Minister, or his principal officials, was ready to consult another Department, where another file was opened and went up and down until the second Minister was ready to consult with the first. Since 1940, however, this hierarchy has broken down. No civil servant now hesitates to consult his 'opposite number' in another Department, by telephone, or by informal discussion, or by having an informal committee. Informal committees are particularly fruitful because the relevant officials can get together and pool their ideas. If, for instance, the politicians of Arcadia, a British base, are asking for self-government, the Colonial Office cannot deal with the problem alone, because the Foreign Office, the Treasury, the Royal Navy, the Army, the Ministry of Aviation (in respect of aerodromes and civil air lines), the Post Office (in respect of cables) must be involved. The Assistant Secretary at the Colonial Office concerned with Arcadia already has the nucleus of a committee in the Principals and Assistant Principals working under him. He can enlarge it by bringing in the equivalent officials, or some of them, from other Departments. More often the equivalent officials are brought in only to make certain that, so far as their problems are concerned, the proposed solution is not objectionable, or that some proviso is inserted to meet their difficulties. In the result, the Assistant Secretary has a tentative solution which he has 'cleared' with all the relevant Departments. It can then be moved up the hierarchy of the Colonial Office until the Secretary of State is ready to take the problem to the Cabinet.

If, however, the Assistant Secretary cannot get agreement with another Department, the problem may have to go higher until it is solved, perhaps by discussion between the Ministers themselves, perhaps even by a Cabinet committee. Under the pre-war system of hierarchy, a proposal was quite likely to get to the Cabinet without being 'cleared' with other Departments. This led to a great deal of congestion at the top, since a Department first knew of a proposal when their Minister received the Cabinet agenda. Accordingly, Cabinet instructions since 1931 have laid down the rule that memoranda are not to be circulated until their subject-matter has been fully examined between the Department from which they emanate, the Treasury, and other Departments concerned. In other words, the proposal must be 'cleared' with other Departments, especially the Treasury, before it comes

177

to the Cabinet. Only if it cannnot be so 'cleared' will a Cabinet committee deal with it. It took some ten years for the Departments to realise that this meant 'clearing' at the lowest possible level, that of Assistant Secretary. It now takes much longer to get a proposal formulated in concrete terms, because so many officials have to be consulted; but there is far less congestion at Cabinet level and Ministers are no longer so oppressed with the volume of work in committee. They have much more to do in their Departments; but they also have more time for it. Moreover, when co-ordination has to be sought at Departmental level, the Minister of State or Parliamentary Secretary can often deputise for the Minister in charge of the Department.

5. INSTRUMENTS OF CO-ORDINATION

It will be seen that the problem of co-ordination does not always require a special institution for its solution. The most important method is that which is purely informal, the day-to-day collaboration between Departments, secured by telephone, personal interview and correspondence. Particularly is this true of the Treasury, whose relations with other Departments are necessarily close. The Permanent Secretary in a Department is appointed by the Prime Minister, acting on the advice of the Permanent Secretary to the Treasury; and though he is a Departmental officer he is also the 'watch-dog' of the Treasury as 'accountant' for all expenditure. He points out to the official concerned with action involving expenditure that the Treasury must be consulted at some stage, and the sooner the better. Close contact is therefore maintained with the Treasury long before any formal submission is made for the consent of 'My Lords'. This informal collaboration is, however, only an example of a daily occurrence. If informal consultations are likely to take long, or if a dispute does arise, the simplest procedure is to appoint *ad hoc* an inter-Departmental committee to settle the principles involved and the boundaries of Departmental jurisdiction. These methods assume that from the beginning the one Department realises that the other may be affected. This is not necessarily so, because the official, running along his own tramlines, may not realise that before he gets to the end of his journey he will reach a junction. Disputes and delay may occur if he has suddenly to put on the brakes. Accordingly, officials are often seconded for service in other Departments as liaison officers, so that they may draw attention to matters affecting the Departments to which they belong.

In other cases a more formal organisation is thought to be necessary. Occasionally an officer, usually a technical officer acting as adviser, serves two Departments. Executive and clerical services were formerly shared by the Colonial Office, and the Commonwealth Relations Office. Occasionally a joint Department, such as the pre-war Department of Overseas Trade or the post-war Department of Technical Co-operation, is set up. Sometimes a Minister without substantial Departmental duties, such as the Lord Privy Seal, the Chancellor of the Duchy of Lancaster, or the Paymaster-General, is asked to co-ordinate Government policy in respect of a group of functions. These devices are often ephemeral. Indeed, one of the most remarkable characteristics of the British system of administration since 1945 has been its fluidity. Every Prime Minister since Attlee has tried experiments, usually with indifferent success, and there has been a constant process of reorganisation at lower levels which, quite often, is not even reported to the House of Commons.

The need for co-ordination at Cabinet level has only recently been recognised because the Cabinet and the Prime Minister are supposed to co-ordinate high policy. In large measure they do; it must be remembered, however, that policies are rarely initiated by the Prime Minister or in the Cabinet. The Prime Minister is a busy person, with little time for original thought. Indeed, it has already been suggested that, in normal times and apart from his capacity as party leader, a good Prime Minister is a good chairman of committees. He ought to be, and usually is, an excellent arbitrator. He can decide and ought to decide Departmental disputes which cannot be settled between the contesting Departments. He ought not only to be available to Ministers when they find themselves at cross-purposes, he ought also to have enough knowledge of what goes on in the Departments to realise when conditions are becoming 'sticky'. He should be able to intervene when action is being held up by difference of opinion, to provide a new demarcation of functions where it can be done without raising questions of principle or demanding legislation, and to shuffle or remove ministers where personal differences stand in the way of effective collaboration. Subject to an exception to be mentioned presently, he has no machinery for developing policy, and though sometimes he may be able to make suggestions as to questions that might be fruitful, he is unlikely to have information adequate enough to permit him to override a Department unless some other Department agrees with him. In other words, he is not in a position to achieve collaboration where co-ordination is most required—in the planning of Government policy as a whole—though he can be a most efficient judge of Departmental differences. So much is this so that some Prime Ministers—Mr Baldwin and Mr Chamberlain, for example—have thought that when demands have been made for better co-ordination they were implicitly a criticism of the Prime Minister. Mr Baldwin thought that the function of a Minister for the Co-ordination of Defence was the settlement of disputes between the Chiefs of Staff; and Mr Chamberlain thought that a Minister for Economic Co-ordination would weaken his own position. In both cases there was a definite misunderstanding. What the critics demanded was not better arbitration but more initiative. They did not complain so much that disputes went on too long, as that in each case the problem needed to be examined by a minister who saw it as a whole and not through the different-coloured spectacles of the several Departments.

The Cabinet is in an even weaker position for this purpose. Four or five elder statesmen or junior ministers can hardly be expected to bring energy and breadth of vision in a Cabinet whose most important members (apart from the Prime Minister) are engaged in solving hosts of immediate questions arising out of pressing administrative needs in their own Departments.

In this respect the situation has fundamentally altered since Peel presided over his Cabinet of nine 'Departmental' and five non-Departmental ministers. The functions of the State controlled by the Cabinet have increased ten-fold or more. The development has been in scope and not merely in depth. The speed of administration has been multiplied since Peel travelled day and night to reach London from Rome in nine days. Leisurely consideration of problems is no longer possible. The difference between Peel and Wilson is the difference between a horse and a 'space rocket'.

In the sphere of defence, the deficiencies of the Cabinet system were made evident during the Crimean War and the Boer War. The War Office (Reconstitution) Committee pointed out in 1904 that

The British Empire is pre-eminently a great Naval, Indian and Colonial Power. There are, nevertheless, no means for co-ordinating defence problems, for dealing with them as a whole, for defining the proper functions of the various elements, and for ensuring that, on the one hand, peace preparations are carried out upon a consistent plan, and, on the other hand, that, in time of emergency, a definite war policy, based upon solid data, can be formulated.

It was accordingly recommended that the Defence Committee of the Cabinet, set up in 1895, be reconstituted as a Committee of Imperial Defence.

The Committee was not, however, a Cabinet committee. Technically, it advised the Prime Minister, who was its only permanent member, and who summoned to each meeting those ministers and officials who were concerned with the items of the agenda. In practice, however, the Treasury, the Foreign Office, the Home Office, the Commonwealth Relations Office, the Colonial Office, the Ministry of Defence, the War Office, the Air Ministry, and the Admiralty were always represented. Moreover the Chiefs of Staff and the Permanent Secretary to the Treasury could for practical purposes be regarded as permanent members. What is perhaps even more important is that, instead of having a secretary drawn for the occasion from a Department, or an official from the Cabinet Office, it had a permanent secretariat to which officers who had been through the Imperial Staff College were attached. Its concern was not so much with Departmental disputes as with the peace-time formulation of plans for war-time operations. Its purpose was to think ahead, to plan in the light of all the information available from nine or more Departments the steps which might have to be taken if war broke out and, with these plans in view, to advise what forces and equipment should be available in the Navy, the Army, and the Air Force. It could take no decisions, but the recommendations of a committee so influential were necessarily received by the Cabinet with very great respect. Moreover, when the Cabinet had decided, the Departments would generally accept the views of the Committee as to what their consequential action should be.

It was inevitably part of the Committee's task to consider the problem of supply. From making recommendations as to the supplies needed to making recommendations for avoiding Departmental competition was but a step. From recommendations relating to armaments to recommendations relating to all supplies required by Departments is only another step. One of its sub-committees, the Supply Board or Principal Supply Officers' Committee, gradually developed a network of committees dealing with the many items which Departments required—oil, motor cars, bicycles, food and the rest.

CABINET GOVERNMENT

Where necessary, supplies were purchased in bulk. Often one Department bought for the rest. This arrangement proved inadequate when the rearmament programme was developed after 1935. The Minister for the Co-ordination of Defence, appointed by Mr Baldwin (to meet the criticism of the slowness of development), spent most of his time co-ordinating supplies. Even this proved insufficient, for he had no machinery under his direct control. In 1939 Mr Chamberlain at last gave way to the demand for a Ministry of Supply, which was made responsible only for supplies to the Army but in fact assumed responsibility for much of the work assumed by the Committees. Mr Churchill created a Ministry of Aircraft Production, and Mr Attlee combined the two Ministries. In 1959 the Ministry of Supply was abolished, its functions being divided between the Ministry of Aviation and the War Office.

Co-ordination among the Defence Departments followed much the same evolution. The task of the Committee of Imperial Defence was to advise the Cabinet on policy and that of the Chiefs of Staff to advise the Committee and thence the Cabinet on strategy. The Prime Minister acted as chairman of both, though it seems that he did not often preside in fact over the Chiefs of Staff. The execution of policy was left to the Service Departments in whose work, it was assumed, the Prime Minister would take a close and consistent interest. There is, however, no evidence that he did so, except in 1916–28, when the Committee of Imperial Defence became the War Cabinet. Between the wars questions like that of the responsibility for the Fleet Air Arm, the control of combined forces, etc., were left outstanding for long periods because the Cabinet could not decide among the experts. Mr Baldwin's Minister for the Co-ordination of Defence did little towards the co-ordination of defence, though he did achieve some co-ordination in respect of supplies. Between 1940 and 1945, however, the conduct of the war was for all essential purposes in the hands of the

Prime Minister. Mr Churchill was most careful not to encroach on the power of the War Cabinet by which all major political questions were decided; but as chairman of the Chiefs of Staff Committee he took strategy into his hands; and in order that there should be no doubt about it he assumed the title of Minister of Defence.

Until 1946, however, there was no Ministry of Defence. The decision to create such a Ministry was due to two factors. First, it was felt that in peace time a Prime Minister, and especially a Labour Prime Minister, could not devote a very large part of his time to defence problems, important though they were, and accordingly that another Minister should be Minister of Defence. Secondly, the experience of the war had shown that a unified defence policy was essential. The Chiefs of Staff had in fact given direct orders, in the Prime Minister's name, to the commanders in the field. It was therefore decided that while the Prime Minister would retain the supreme responsibility for defence and the Service Ministers should retain the responsibility for the administration of their Services in accordance with the general policy laid down by the Cabinet, there should be a Minister of Defence responsible for:

(1) the apportionment of available resources of man-power and raw materials among the Services in accordance with the strategic policy laid down by the Defence Committee;

(2) the settlement of questions of general administration on which a common policy was desirable; and

(3) the administration of inter-Service organisations, such as Combined Operations Headquarters and the Joint Intelligence Bureau.

After 1951 the functions of the Ministry substantially increased, particularly through arrangements made by Sir Anthony Eden in 1956. By this time the Defence Committee, which had replaced the Committee of Imperial Defence in 1946, had apparently become a Cabinet Committee, advised by the Chiefs of Staff. Under the reforms of 1956 the Chiefs of Staff Committee was strengthened by the appointment of a service officer as chairman. At the same time the co-ordinating functions of the Ministry of Defence were extended to the Ministry of Supply, which was a 'fourth service department' until it was abolished in 1959. Even in 1951 the disappearance of the service departments was foreseen, though it was not brought about until 1964, when the Admiralty, the War Office and the Air Ministry disappeared. The three services remain, and there are separate Ministers of Defence for the Royal Navy, the Army and the Royal Air Force. They are, however, subordinate to the Secretary of State for Defence, who has replaced the Minister of Defence. At the same time it was declared (Cmnd. 2097) that it was necessary

'to consider major questions of defence policy not only in purely military terms but also in relation to Britain's foreign and economic policy'.

Accordingly, the Defence Committee of the Cabinet was replaced by a Defence and Overseas Policy Committee, presided over by the Prime Minister, and including the Foreign Secretary, the Chancellor of the Exchequer, the Home Secretary, the Secretaries of State for Commonwealth Relations and the Colonies, and the Secretary of State for Defence. The Chief of the Defence Staff and the Chiefs of Staff, and civil servants, would attend as required.

In civil matters there has been something of the same evolution. Town and country planning, which was mainly the concern of the Ministries of Health and Transport before the war, was handed over to a Ministry of Town and Country Planning in 1943, though it has now reverted to the Ministry of Housing and Local Government, which has superseded the old Ministry of Health. It was, however, decided in 1945 that housing policy could not be handed over to a Ministry of Housing because the collaboration of several Departments would still be required, and a new Ministry would merely add one to the list. The social insurance schemes, formerly operated by the Ministry of Labour, the Ministry of Health, and the Board of Customs and Excise have passed, via the now defunct Ministry of National Insurance, to the control of the Ministry of Social Security (1966). This Ministry also administers the payment of what was formerly known as national assistance to unemployed persons without claims to covenanted benefits or to needy pensioners.

Whether economic problems can be tackled in the same way is one of the outstanding questions. Preparation for defence is a comparatively simple problem because, though the whole population will be involved if war breaks out, the peace-time requirement is simply a highly skilled professional machine. Economic planning, on the other hand, requires the active collaboration of the whole population. By analogy the need for an 'Economic General Staff' is often mentioned, but, whereas the Chiefs of Staff give orders to their subordinates in the three professional Services, the Economic General Staff would have to give orders to, or at least secure the active collaboration of, managers and workers in countless enterprises, as well as millions of consumers. Further, the actions of other peoples which will affect our defence problems can be forecast with reasonable accuracy, but nobody can forecast what wars, floods, droughts, epidemics, strikes, lock-outs, economic policies, political changes, and so on, will affect our economic problems in the next few years.

One simple example will suffice. Our bread supply is dependent on wheat supplies from Canada, which are dependent upon adequate snow falling on the prairies, political conditions in Canada, the dollar exchange, and so on. But our supplies are also dependent on the world demand for wheat; and among the many events which might affect that demand is war or civil war in Burma, because if Burma's rice supplies are reduced the demands for wheat will increase. Since this is one example among thousands, it is obvious that economic planning cannot be a precise science. It was clear before the war of 1939–45 that much more could be done towards collecting the necessary information and working out, if not a long-term policy, at least a series of financial propositions whose detailed application would have to be varied from year to year and indeed from month to month.

In 1925 Mr Baldwin appointed a Committee for Civil Research which was intended to do for social policy what the Department of Scientific and Industrial Research did for scientific investigation. It examined a few problems of no great significance but did not tackle any of the main economic difficulties. In 1930 Mr MacDonald converted it into an Economic Advisory Council composed of Cabinet Ministers and economic and other experts. Such a body must necessarily differ in opinion even over 'academic' questions of no immediate political concern; it could hardly be expected to reach unanimity on the economic aspects of current politics. Though some of its sub-committees produced reports, there were years in which the Council did not meet. Mr MacDonald's Government had to face a particularly difficult economic problem, the depression which began in the United States in 1929 and spread to England to such a degree that it destroyed the Government. There is no evidence that the Economic Advisory Council played any part in solving or even failing to solve this problem, which was in fact referred to a committee of civil servants with Sir John Anderson as chairman.

Before war broke out in 1939 it was felt that serious attention had to be paid to the economic problem. Obviously the economic resources of the country had to be 'mobilised'—to use the current catchphrase—to enable the maximum war effort to be produced. It was decided to establish an Interdepartmental Committee on Economic Policy, with Lord Stamp as chairman, and with a number of economists as advisers, the Lord President of the Council being responsible to Parliament. This 'Stamp Survey' produced a large number of very valuable studies, though there is no evidence that they were adequately used. Partly as a consequence of this organisation and partly independently, a staff of economists and statisticians was built up at the Cabinet Office as the 'Central Economic Information Service'. Later, this was split into the Central Statistical Office, which remains at the Cabinet Office, and the group of economists, who wandered far before they reached the promised land of the Treasury.

Mr Churchill concentrated on the conduct of the war and left the 'home front' to his colleagues. Responsibility for the economic side of the home front he placed, somewhat curiously, on the Lord President of the Council, who therefore assumed control of the economic staff at the Cabinet Office. The explanation lay partly in the fact that the Lord President was a member of the War Cabinet without heavy departmental duties, and partly in the fact that Sir John Anderson had given much thought to these problems before the war. The Lord President presided over a ministerial committee which met weekly to survey and settle on behalf of the War Cabinet such problems as those of distribution of manpower, allocation of raw materials, use of shipping, etc. The Economic Section of the Cabinet Office kept in close touch with the Departments with a view to providing the material for and giving advice to the Lord President on these and other economic matters. It is generally agreed that this arrangement worked with remarkable success, but several features, not all of which would be characteristic of peacetime government, need to be emphasised.

In the first place, the objective was plain and unambiguous. The task of the economist was to supply the means by which the armed forces of the Allies might be enabled to attain superiority over their enemies. This no doubt explains in large part what has been called 'the impressive war-time harmony of economists'.[1] There was no mixture of politics and

[1] Quoted by Sir John Anderson in *The Organization of Economic Studies in Relation to the Problems of Government* (Oxford, 1947) from which much of the above has been taken.

economics as there is inevitably in peace-time policies, where people's ideas both about objectives and about methods necessarily differ.

In the second place, and largely as a consequence, economic policy was a secondary and subordinate issue, since the people generally were prepared to submit to controls and deprivations in order to win the war, whereas in peace time it becomes the primary issue, since it is assumed (rightly or wrongly) that the electors are concerned fundamentally with advancing their own individual well-being. The economists were, so to speak, allowed to run their own show because economic policy was a technical issue in such conditions, whereas in peace time it is an issue on which politicians take sides.

In the third place, and again partly consequentially, the Government could rely on the fullest collaboration from the economic groups, including private industry and the trade unions, most of which were willing to subordinate their sectional interests in order to further the war effort. Such conditions would not obtain in peace time because some groups, at least, would deny that the Government's objectives, whether it was a Conservative Government or a Labour Government, were really in the national interest.

Sir Oliver Franks pointed out in three admirable lectures[1] that the United Kingdom obtained certain advantages through this war-time experience. First, the Government (which means not only the politicians but also the civil servants) gained much knowledge of the manner in which trade and industry function and of the people who function in them. Secondly, the Government Departments acquired knowledge of the methods needed for central planning, even though it be true that peace-time planning is very much more complicated than that of war. Thirdly, the men who control trade and industry have a much better knowledge

[1] *Central Planning and Control in War and Peace* (London School of Economics, 1947).

of the way in which Government works and of the aims which governments pursue. Fourthly, the nation as a whole became accustomed to the principle that private interests must be subordinated to the national good.

In 1944 in the White Paper on Employment Policy (which was evidently produced by the Economic Section and was, so to speak, a formal acceptance of the doctrines of Lord Keynes), the Government accepted the doctrine of Full Employment, a doctrine which implied that the monetary, fiscal and expenditure policy of the Government would be so planned as to maintain a close relationship between the supply of and the demand for labour. If certain other factors, such as the need for regulating conditions of work, housing and town planning, standards of products, etc. and also for providing a full range of social services, be excluded, this may be regarded as the highest common factor of agreed economic policy. Beyond it, the parties have different policies, those of the Conservative party emphasising freedom and initiative for competitive industry and those of the Labour party emphasising national ownership and control in the interest of the worker and the consumer.

Since there is a large measure of agreement (which, incidentally, confirms the opinion expressed earlier in this book that there is not a fundamental divergence between Government and Opposition) the Government machinery has to allow for a large measure of planning. Since the Labour party won the election of 1945 it had, in theory at least, to allow for an even larger measure.

For a time Mr Attlee continued the war-time organisation. For reasons which have not been explained, but probably because the Lord President of the Council was fully engaged in managing the House of Commons and because Labour party policy must necessarily emphasise economic planning, he decided in 1947 to establish a Ministry of Economic Planning, though the then President of the Board of Trade, Sir Stafford Cripps, assumed the responsibility in addition to his other duties. In 1948, however, Sir Stafford Cripps became Chancellor of the Exchequer, and he then carried into the Treasury the functions that he had performed as Minister of Economic Planning.

The Central Statistical Office remains part of the Cabinet Office, and it should be said that as a result of the war-time experience a much fuller and better statistical service is now available to the Government. It prepares in particular the Monthly Digest of Statistics and the Annual Abstract of Statistics, which are essential for an adequate understanding of the problems of government. Before the war only an Annual Abstract was published, and then under the control of an inter-departmental committee. It also produces an annual survey of the National Income and Expenditure of the United Kingdom, which is a fundamental document for all those who can claim to speak on economic policy.

The Central Statistical Office is not, however, a policy-forming Department. Under the Conservative Governments of 1951–64 the responsibility for this function rested with the Treasury, which had a small 'Economic Section' of economic advisers. The Economic Planning Board, set up by the Labour Government in 1947, remained in being for some years, but it was presided over not by a full-time Chief Planning Officer with wide industrial experience, but by one of the Permanent Secretaries to the Treasury; and most of its members were senior civil servants. In 1962, however, it was replaced by the National Economic Development Council, whose task was 'to examine the economic performance of the nation with particular concern for plans for the future in both the private and the public sectors of industry; to consider together what are the obstacles to quicker growth, what can be done to improve efficiency, and whether the best use is being made of our resources; and to seek agreement upon ways of improving economic performance, competitive power, and efficiency...' Under the Conservative Government the Chancellor of the Exchequer presided and the

President of the Board of Trade and the Minister of Labour were members, together with representatives of public corporations, private industry, and trade unions. It was given a full-time staff.

On the formation of the Labour Government in 1964 economic planning was taken out of the Treasury and was vested in the 'First Secretary of State and Minister for Economic Affairs'. He was given the responsibility of framing and supervising the plan for economic development, and for the general co-ordination of action to implement the plan, including in particular policies for industry, regional development, incomes and prices, and economic development. The Government thought that there was a continuing need for an outside body to discuss the Government's economic plans and contribute to their formulation, to discuss more generally policies for economic growth, particularly those depending on the understanding and co-operation of industry, and to provide a channel of communication with individual industries. The N.E.D.C. was therefore reconstituted and its functions modified.

First, the assumption on which a National Plan is built is that there will be a consistency in economic policy which is foreign to the parliamentary system. Economic policy is at the centre of political controversy and must be adapted to changes in public opinion. It cannot be expected that a Conservative Government will follow a plan produced by a Labour Government or vice versa. What is more, any Government must mould its policy to meet public opinion and keep itself in power. It follows from the logic of the parliamentary system that if any part of the plan seems likely to lose votes at the next election it will not be carried out. This argument suggests that a plan would be no more than a norm from which any Government would feel at liberty to depart at any moment and perhaps for all time.

Secondly, a National Plan cannot be carried out by Governmental action alone. It requires the collaboration of industrialists, workers and consumers. No doubt there can be 'controls', as there were during the war; but the success of those controls lay in the fact that everybody recognised their necessity as instruments for winning the war. It would be unreasonable to expect industrialists to give full collaboration in the operation of controls when they disagreed with their need and with the principles on which the plan was based. Nor is the danger only from them, as is sometimes assumed. Trade unionists have learned to assume that they are entitled to use their collective power to raise wages and better their conditions of work. It was not easy for the Attlee Government, with whose political views most of them were in sympathy, to persuade them to alter their conditions and to 'freeze wages'. Again, consumers are apt to assume that they are entitled to spend their money on what they want and not on the commodities which, according to the plan, ought to be produced, imported and sold. The workers and the consumers are the great mass of the electorate and, as long as the preparation of alternative policies is permissible they might, for instance, decide to turn out a Government which did not produce or permit enough sweets, tobacco, beer, films, fashions and football pools. This argument might lead to the conclusion that the State must either become at once completely socialist and totalitarian, as in the Soviet Union, or have no plan at all; but this ignores the possibility of a very elastic plan which allows considerable adaptation to changing fashions and varying opinion. It does suggest, however, that planning is a difficult art, and that it is easier to produce a plan which will fail than one which will succeed.

Thirdly, as Sir Oliver Franks had pointed out[1], the execution of a plan cannot be the business of a Department of Planning; it must be carried out by all, or nearly all, the Departments. Who is to be the watch dog, and how can we be sure of his barking whenever some decision is taken,

[1] *Op. cit.* p. 49.

perhaps by an Assistant Secretary, which does not conform with the plan? Nor will it be enough to bark. The dog must be in a position to bite if need be. The answer is, of course, that we should have to educate not only our masters, in the old Victorian sense, but also our servants, and we might have to ask whether the old assumption that a man or woman trained in Classics or Mathematics or even 'Philosophy, Politics and Economics' is necessarily capable of putting a plan into execution.

CHAPTER VIII

BRITISH DEMOCRACY

I. GOVERNMENT AND OPINION

The fact which emerges most clearly from the survey in this book is the close relation between the policies followed by the Government and the general ideas of the majority of the electorate. It is a consequence of the simple principles upon which the British Constitution is based. The Government governs because it has a majority in the House of Commons. It possesses that majority because the party which it leads secured a majority of seats at the last general election. The parties are not mere electioneering organisations, as they tend to be in Canada and the United States, but are truly based upon competing political principles. In preferring one party to another, therefore, the electorate not only prefers one Government to another but prefers one line of policy to another. Its choice is of course made at infrequent intervals, but always the Government in power has the prospect of having to appeal to the electorate at no very distant date. If it wishes to remain in power it must continue to receive the support of a majority. It must be able to base a successful appeal on its past record. It must be able to explain away its mistakes and emphasise its achievements. Every mistake is an argument against it and every achievement an argument for it. Therefore it must not make obvious mistakes, and its achievements must be such as will meet the elector's approval. Since in fact the division of support between the two major parties is extremely small, any Government must have profound respect for movements of opinion. Nor can it fail to be aware of such movements, for every member of the House of Commons is in close touch with his constituency and is aware of the currents that tend to lose him votes. He will lose votes from every unpopular action by his leaders because he is elected not on his personality nor on his political record but on his party label. A vote against the Government is a vote against him. Accordingly, he expresses in the House or in the lobbies the fear that the Government policy induces in him. He sounds the alarm in the House when the bell begins to ring in his constituency. What is more, if Parliament proves insensitive, there are now 'public opinion polls' to frighten the electioneers in party headquarters.

If there were any doubt about this analysis before the war, there can be none now. With the aid of election studies and public opinion polls it has been possible to watch public opinion swaying from side to side and party policies changing in harmony. 'Controls', nationalisation, planning, Suez, Nyasaland, the H-bomb, Hola Camp, inflation, housing and old age pensions have been straws in the wind which have enabled the parties, without admitting their political mistakes, to change direction through angles wide enough to change the party 'images'. At the general election of 1964 the electors' mental travail was almost painful to watch.

Some qualifications must nevertheless be made to the general statement made above. In the first place it must be made clear that the electorate and the people are not quite the same body. Since 1949 the correlation between them has been greater than ever before, partly because double votes were extinguished and 'one man, one vote' brought into operation by the Representation of the People Act, 1948, for the first time, and partly because there has been a sufficient redistribution of seats to make one vote of almost equal electoral value. Nevertheless, the people who vote are not quite the same as the people who might vote. The results of local elections, for instance, give little guide to the results of parliamentary elections, not only because the issues are different, but also because at a local election 50 per cent is a good poll, whereas the average poll in parliamentary elections is 75 per cent. Even so, the other 25 per cent help to form public opinion. Indeed, the man who talks loudest or most convincingly in the club or the pub may not vote at all.

Secondly, the power of public opinion can operate only where there is a powerful party system which gives the electors a real alternative. In Great Britain this condition is satisfied; for though it is true that many constituencies never change their allegiance, a slight change of opinion swings the marginal constituencies and hence changes the Government. It has not been entirely satisfied in Northern Ireland, where the strength of the Unionist party (a reflection of the opposition to nationalist Ireland) has prevented a real choice.

Thirdly, our system of representation produces the result that the size of a majority in the House of Commons may bear little relationship to the size of the majority in the country. In 1935, for instance, the Conservative party and its dependents gained, allowing for uncontested seats, about $54 \cdot 5$ per cent of the votes but 70 per cent of the seats. In 1945 the Labour party gained about 40 per cent of the votes but 61 per cent of the seats. Even in 1959, when the Conservative party won a large majority, it had less than half the votes cast. The consequences have been discussed in Chapter II, where it is suggested that the advantages of proportional representation are not so great as the disadvantages. In any case, proportional representation usually means not government by the people but government by groups. The argument on which this part of the chapter is based is that because the Government has a majority and because it wishes to retain that majority it is and must be extremely susceptible to changes of opinion in the constituencies. In all probability a coalition based on groups would be far less susceptible, because movements of opinion would be obscured and political crises would depend very largely on personal sympathies and antipathies. It is important that every section of opinion should have its instrument of expression, but not that it should be proportionately represented in the House.

This bring us to the fourth point, that the opinions which weigh most heavily are not the large sections but what may be called the 'marginal' opinion, represented by the floating vote. The nature and size of that vote have already been discussed. The result is to emphasise the lower middle-class opinion in the suburbs and suburbanised county districts. It is of course true that no party dares to antagonise the main body of its supporters, but at present neither can gain a majority without capturing the marginal votes. No representative system can avoid this result. Proportional representation, in fact, would exaggerate it by placing the balance of the Constitution in the hands of an organised group at least as capable of using it for the personal ambitions of its leaders as for the benefit of the marginal voters. Nor has any other system avoided the result. Even in presidential elections in the United States the 'key' States are known, and the electoral college system has enormously exaggerated it. Moreover, combined with the irresponsibility of the executive, the strength of minorities has led to the practice of the organised lobby and the pork-barrel.

Finally, it must be confessed that public opinion is apt to be swayed not by reason and knowledge but by emotion and propaganda. The parties are in fact vast propaganda machines. On the one hand the Conservative party beats the mystical drum of patriotism and on the other hand the Labour party plays the shrill fife of social sympathy. This is a characteristic of all democracies. It is, however, still more a characteristic of dictatorships, as those who are old enough to remember Hitler and Mussolini know only too well. The difference is that in a democracy the elector can choose between the drum and the fife, whereas in the dictatorships he had to choose between the drum (or the trombone) and the rubber truncheon. The result in Great Britain is that the ordinary elector has a good deal of suspicion of all the instruments of the political orchestra. He is apt to 'confound their politics' (in more Anglo-Saxon language) and turn to the racing results. He retains enough interest to vote, but votes according to what he believes to be his interest. In consequence he is accused by the Marxists of not being 'politically conscious'. It is true that he is not conscious of the Marxist interpretation of history and hates class war as much as he hates imperialist war; but he is fully conscious either of the importance of 'working-class solidarity', in which case he votes Labour, or of the importance of 'financial stability', in which case he votes Conservative. There are, of course, cross-currents, especially among the middle classes. Roman Catholics generally believe that there is some connection between socialism and atheism; the Church of England generally induces a mild Conservatism; the Free Churches are apt to be radical, especially in Wales and Scotland; and intellectual movements help to sway the marginal votes. John Stuart Mill's rationalist assumptions are largely false, but the British voter has a sound and steady empiricism which he calls 'common sense'. Moreover, since television invaded most electors' homes the political parties have had to dispense with their orchestras. Nothing would be funnier than Sir Alec Douglas Home or Mr Wilson tub-thumping on television. They and their supporters have to appear as reasonable men and women appealing to reasonable men and women.

It is sometimes said that the Government in power is able to delude the people by neglecting to give unpalatable information and making comfortable forecasts which it knows to be false. Emphasis is laid on a speech by Mr Baldwin on 12 November 1936, in which, with 'appalling frankness', he confessed that in 1933 and 1934 he had failed to give a lead for rearmament because of the probable electoral consequence. There was a by-election at Fulham in the autumn of 1933, when the Government lost a seat by 7,000 votes 'on no issue but the pacifist'.

Supposing I had gone to the country and said that Germany was rearming and that we must rearm, does anybody think that this pacific democracy would have rallied to that cry at that moment? I cannot think of anything that would have made the loss of the election from my point of view more certain.

Mr Baldwin went on to say that 'the country itself learned by certain events that took place during the winter of 1934–35 what the perils might be' and in 1935 the government secured from the electorate 'a mandate for doing a thing that no one, 12 months before, would have believed possible'. In fact, however, rearmament was not the main issue at the general election of 1935. Mr Neville Chamberlain had wished it to be so, but had been overruled by the party officials. The party manifesto therefore made as strong a point of 'the establishment of a settled peace' through the League of Nations as of the need for rearmament. Even if Mr Baldwin's confession related to a hypothetical election in 1933, it is plain that there was a suppression of vital information because it might have had an adverse effect on his party's electoral prospects; and it is also clear that the danger was deliberately minimised at the general election of 1935 lest votes be lost. What is more, the case was exceptional only because the danger—as the electors discovered in 1940 —was so great. No election manifesto contains a cool appraisal of past actions and future policies. Each party claims that it has all the virtues and its opponents all the vices.

The example shows some limitations of public control. In the first place, it is not easy to create a public opinion at all in matters which do not affect people's lives immediately and closely. Foreign policy demands a knowledge of people, events and tendencies which the ordinary person does not possess and which, indeed, he cannot easily acquire. The foreign news in the papers is seldom good because cabled news is expensive and it is even more expensive to keep special correspondents in foreign countries. What news there is is not read very carefully—and this is another reason to justify the tendency of the newspapers to keep it to a minimum. Yet difficulties usually arise in foreign affairs not because of isolated events or decisions but because of general tendencies of policy—the Suez episode of 1956 was so very odd that it may be said to have proved the rule. There are, for instance, at least three versions of the British policy which ended in 1939 with the outbreak of war. Sir Winston Churchill, in *The Gathering Storm*, produced a strong condemnation of the National Government for not following the policy which he had himself consistently supported, of increasing armaments and resisting the growing aggression of the dictators. An equally strong condemnation might, however, be produced by a Labour party supporter on the entirely opposite ground that the National Government had, from the time of the Japanese invasion of Manchuria, failed to make adequate use of the machinery for collective security provided by the League of Nations. Presumably a case could be made, and in some degree Mr Keith Feiling has made it in his *Life of Neville Chamberlain*, for the policy which the Government did in fact follow. The point is, however, that it is difficult if not impossible to say that any particular decision of the Government was right or wrong, because the context in which the decision had to be taken was in some measure created by the Government itself. If public opinion is to be effective in foreign policy it must follow the whole course of that policy, and not merely express an opinion when it seems to be producing unsatisfactory results, as in 1939.

Actually there has been no period in our recent history when public opinion paid so much attention to foreign policy as in the period 1933 to 1939. In large measure this was due to the antics of the mountebanks who governed Italy and Germany; but it was also due to the consistent propaganda of the League of Nations Union and the Labour party. There is no doubt that, at least from 1933 to 1936, it was against the

Government. It is here that Mr Baldwin's 'confession' becomes relevant. Finding public opinion against it in 1933–35, the Government neither changed its published policy nor tried to change public opinion. Instead, it followed a practice which can only be described as dishonest, by continuing to give lip-service to collective security and at the same time beginning, not very efficiently, the process of rearmament. It must of course be said that there may have been difficulty in using the language needed for convincing public opinion. Speeches on foreign affairs are heard not only by British electors but also by foreign powers. It was one thing for a lone crusader like Mr Winston Churchill to attack foreign governments; it was another for His Majesty's Government to do so. Still, Mr Neville Chamberlain was prepared to go to the country on rearmament in 1935; it was the fear of the electors, not the fear of foreign governments, which made the Cabinet decide otherwise.

Further, the episode illustrates the difficulty of securing the enforcement of public opinion in foreign policy. As has been said above, the process of government in foreign affairs is not one of taking individual decisions but a continuing process of taking connected decisions. The nation was led to support 'appeasement' in 1938 because Mr Chamberlain's previous policy had led to it, just as a large part of the nation was led to support the Boer War because the previous policy of Mr Joseph Chamberlain had led to it. In other words, even when the foreign policy approved by the people is clear (and this rarely happens) its execution lies in the hands of the Government, which can sabotage that policy, and compel the adoption of its own, by carrying out the policy inefficiently. The only remedy of public opinion is to throw out the Government at the next opportunity, and meanwhile other political issues may become dominant. The Balfour Government went down with a crash in 1905 and the Chamberlain Government disappeared in 1940, but it can hardly be said that the former was due to Mr Joseph

Chamberlain's policy after 1896 or the latter to Mr Baldwin's 'confession'.

2. DEMOCRACY AND LIBERTY

With all these qualifications, it is still true that the relation between Government and opinion in Great Britain is very close. It could not be so close but for one factor of which, perhaps, not enough has been said in this book—the general acceptance of the principles of civil liberty. The fact that so little has been said on this subject is in itself evidence of the generality of the acceptance. Civil liberty is so fundamental that a description of it might almost be taken as read. In these days, however, old heresies masquerade under new names. To allow the attacks upon the principles of liberty to go by default might be to give the impression not, as is the case, that they are not worthy of being answered, but that they cannot be answered. Nor would it be proper to conclude a survey of the British Constitution without an explanation of the great principles for which the peoples of these islands and of their colonies in North America fought and died.

Emphasis is rightly placed on the laws and institutions which protect liberty in this country. What is less often realised is that liberty is a consequence not of laws and institutions but of an attitude of mind. Laws can be broken and institutions subverted. A people can be forcibly enslaved but it cannot be 'forced to be free'. It becomes free because it desires to be free, and it remains free because it so intends. Civil and religious liberty came to Great Britain as a lesson drawn from bitter experience. The lesson was first learned in the sphere of religious liberty, though religious and political liberty could not then be clearly distinguished. Those who believe that they have found truth and that those who spurn it have souls in danger of eternal damnation may reasonably think it their duty to stamp out heresy. Roman Catholics, the Reformed Church of England, the Scottish

Covenanters, the English 'Saints', had their own brands of truth and their own standards of heresy. Oliver Cromwell, the statesman who had to govern a multitude of sects, might make fine speeches on toleration. His secretary, John Milton, might in *Areopagitica* write the finest defence of liberty in the English language. They were, however, in advance of their time. Not until the 'age of reason' in the eighteenth century was it recognised that truth, if there was such a thing, was many-sided and that any Protestant might have learned a portion of it. Not until after Culloden, when Romanism ceased to be sedition, could Roman Catholics begin to worship in peace, and not until 1829 were their main legal disabilities swept away. Even the age of reason could not accept agnosticism or atheism as arguable propositions, and the political disabilities of Jews and dissenters were not all abolished until late in the nineteenth century.

In the meantime the connection between religion and politics had become less close. Church patronage was to Walpole a means of keeping himself in power. Bolingbroke could be a Deist (though in private), seek to lead the party of 'Church and King', and hold treasonable converse with a Romanist Pretender. A political leader ran the risk of impeachment not because of his religious opinions, but because he had lost his majority. Not until late in the eighteenth century was political opposition pardonable, and even Charles James Fox was struck off the roll of the Privy Council.

It is true that long before the eighteenth century civil liberty in the narrow sense had been established. A host of foreign commentators, among them Montesquieu, Voltaire and de Lolme, bore testimony to the freedom that prevailed in England. A conflict against the King and the King's religion was a conflict for the liberty and the property of the individual. The Court of Star Chamber went the way of the Court of High Commission. The abolition of newspaper licensing was almost an accident. The Parliament that tried to exclude James II from the throne passed the Habeas Corpus Act. The Bill of Rights which declared the abdication of James II dealt with jurors and excessive bail. The Act of Settlement which transferred the Crown to a more remote Protestant line provided for the independence of judges. Toleration was being erected into a principle, but it is not too much to say that civil liberty was gradually established as a series of empirical solutions of problems raised by the general and religious opinions of the Stuarts.

The result was, however, clear. The great Whig improvisations became the great Whig principles. All were in danger when the French Revolution of 1789 sent the Old Corps into the arms of the Tories. Charles James Fox and the second Earl Grey fought a gallant rearguard action, and countless almost unknown heroes resisted in the battle which culminated in the failure of the Six Acts. Earl Grey was carried along on the rising tide of the new middle class, and the Whig principles of 1689 became the principles of both political parties.

To explain what these principles are is no easy matter because their precise connotation varies with the functions of the State. For much of the nineteenth century they meant *laissez-faire*, and they are frequently asserted in that extreme form even to-day, when all parties are more or less collectivist. Even the most concrete application can rarely be stated without qualification. To say that 'no man can be kept imprisoned except on the orders of a court', for instance, is false, because lunatics, mental deficients, persons suffering from infectious disease, and so on, may be detained without their consent. It must again be emphasised that liberty is the consequence of an attitude of mind rather than of precise rules. It involves insistence on the idea that the action of the State must be directed to achieve the happiness and prosperity of all sections of the community, without regard to wealth, social prestige, 'race' or religion. It recognises that the advantage of the many ought not to be purchased at the expense of the suffering of the few. It stresses the autonomy of the individual without asserting that a substantial degree of regulation may not be desirable. It forbids anti-social activity without making the individual a slave tied to a machine.

These are generalities which give infinite scope for differences of opinion as to their application. If they are applied too widely they tend to the creation of a social and economic anarchy because they make the individual free to be enslaved. If the qualifications are interpreted too widely, they make the individual a slave to a machine. Between the extremes is an area in which true friends of liberty may hold different opinions without denying the essential idea. Within that area British political parties formulate their programmes.

Certain institutions are, however, clearly necessary. The first is an honest and impartial administration of justice. That has certainly been attained. No suggestion of corruption is ever made against our judges. They may often be mistaken; their remedies may sometimes be unavailable to poor men because they are too costly; but they enjoy a reputation for probity which many nations have cause to envy. Moreover, they are independent of political control and political influence. They take orders from nobody except Parliament and superior courts. Though sometimes they have been appointed (more often in the remoter past than in the past generation) because of their political success, they do their best to be impartial, and they would openly and forcibly spurn any attempt at political pressure.

It is necessary, however, that there should be not only impartiality in the judges but also impartiality in the laws. This does not mean, as some have assumed, that all laws must apply equally to everyone. There must be special laws for bankers, and not everyone is a banker. What it does mean is that the laws must not make irrelevant distinctions. The law of banking must apply equally to all bankers, whether they are Jews or Gentiles, Conservatives or Socialists, Roman Catholics or Quakers, moderate drinkers or total abstainers. The more general the evil to be avoided or the advantage to be gained, the more general the law. The law of murder or of theft can make no distinctions between peers and poets, rich men and poor, public servants and private employees. On the other hand, generality and impartiality do not mean that special classes of persons like publicans or public officials may not have special obligations imposed upon them. Nor does it mean that individual owners may not be deprived of their property or have special restrictions imposed upon it in the general interest. In such a case, one property owner is distinguished from another for relevant and not irrelevant considerations like 'race', religion or political opinion. Since there is a differentiation, however, it is recognised that compensation must be paid. In other words, what this application of the general idea means is that deprivation of liberty or property must be by 'due process of law'. In particular, 'race', religion and political opinion are irrelevant except in so far as they tend to promote disorder or subvert our democratic Constitution.

The impartiality of laws is not maintained except by the impartiality of their application. The impartiality of the judges is one means by which this is secured. So far as judges are competent and judicial procedure is appropriate, therefore, the application should be left to the Courts. Frequently, however, judges are incompetent because expert knowledge is required and judicial procedure is inappropriate because its cost and formality hinder proper investigation and prevent poor persons from protecting their interests. Judges cannot administer the law of education; judicial procedure is not an appropriate instrument for determining whether it is reasonable to refuse to allow a house to be built by the side of a main road; the judicial procedure is too dilatory and costly to determine whether John Smith is genuinely in search of work. The greater the activity of the State, therefore, the greater the need for honest and impartial administration. Here, too, the British Constitution teaches more lessons than it can learn. Its success is in part due to the civil service which has already been described; in part it is due to the system of local government which is outside the scope of this book. It is, however, also due to the control which the courts exercise over public authorities. This system cannot be praised without qualification, because the methods have been dilatory and expensive, and they have not always been applied with proper understanding of the problems involved. Nevertheless, the courts have set their faces sternly against partiality and corruption, and they have insisted that 'justice must not only be done but must be seen to be done'.

Of the technical methods by which these functions have been exercised there is no space to write. Every Englishman has heard of *habeas corpus*, because it has sometimes lain near the centre of political controversy. He ought also to know about *mandamus*, prohibition and *certiorari*. Nor is this all. Justice and liberty are not maintained only through remedies with Latin names. It is the ordinary administration of civil and criminal law and the interpretation of administrative statutes which matters most. There are defects with which every lawyer is familiar. There are some methods adopted elsewhere, notably by the French, which might be adopted here. The law is in many parts still the 'ungodly jumble' of which Carlyle spoke. Yet this certainly English (and Scottish) law does provide, that no man is penalised because he is a Jew, or poor, or without political or social influence, or because he belongs to a party, or because he has unusual notions about a future life.

Nevertheless, we must return to our main point. All this is not so because of technical devices and peculiar rules of law. The law is what Parliament provides, and it is in Parliament that the focus of our liberties must be found. Civil liberty is a consequence of political liberty, and political liberty is the result of a long evolution. The freedom of debate in Parliament asserted by the Bill of Rights is one of the most important political principles. The symbol of liberty is Her Majesty's Opposition. This too requires a background of liberty. Without free elections there can be no true parliamentary freedom—though it was only in 1872 that Parliament was convinced that in order to be free voting must be secret. Without freedom of speech, freedom of public meeting, and freedom of association there cannot be free elections. These liberties are not absolute, for freedom to work the Constitution cannot imply freedom to subvert the Constitution, and there is not always agreement on the extent of the qualifications. Nevertheless, the principles are accepted. Moreover, it is because they are accepted that they remain. A Government with a majority in both Houses would find no technical difficulty in sweeping them away.

It is clear, therefore, that the source of our liberty is not in laws or institutions, but in the spirit of a free people. It is the more firmly founded because it expanded so slowly. The liberty for which our forefathers took up arms was a very limited liberty—freedom for a reformed Church, freedom from royal absolutism, parliamentary freedom. For the rest, liberty has 'broadened down from precedent to precedent'.

3. IS IT A DEMOCRACY?

In 1940 an American citizen wrote to *The Spectator* from Seattle, Washington, to explain why many American citizens were at that time isolationist. His argument included the assertion that Britain was not a democracy in his sense of the term.

If what you mean by democracy was the system practised in England just before the war, you will find many here in America who will dissent to your use of the term. I, as an American, do not consider equal justice for all as denoting democracy, or even equable political representation. Democracy must stand on a different basis from something which is grudgingly given by a conciliatory upper class to classes which are hard pressing it. Democracy must stand on the ground of the most common and least privileged of the people composing a country. It must first be of the people before it can be by it or for it. Therefore you do not touch us when you say that you are fighting for democracy. You are not fighting for our kind of democracy.

The statement is worth quoting because it represents a point of view that is not to be found only on the shores of Puget Sound. That we have not an egalitarian democracy will be readily agreed; that the United States or the State of Washington has an egalitarian democracy will not be agreed so readily. Comparisons are odious, and few are experienced enough to be able to make them. If it is true, as this book alleges, that there is a close correspondence between the actions of the Government and the opinions of an electorate containing all 'the most common and least privileged of the people', it is difficult and, indeed, impossible to assert that this is not a democracy. If it is true, as this chapter alleges, that British liberty—not merely 'equable political representation' and 'equal justice for all'—rests on the spirit of a free people, it is difficult to understand how free peoples everywhere can fail to sympathise with it.

The sting of the statement lies, however, in the phrase 'grudgingly given by a conciliatory upper class to classes which are hard pressing it'. It would be easy to retort with a *tu quoque*. An American citizen in far-off Seattle may be pardoned if he misunderstands who are this 'conciliatory upper class'. It certainly did not come over with William the Conqueror. It is not the descendants of those who killed each other in the Wars of the Roses. It is not the 'new nobility' of the Tudors. It is not the landowners of the eighteenth century, nor even the manufacturers of the nineteenth. At its worst it is no worse than the bankers of Wall Street, the steel kings of Pittsburgh, or the lumber kings of Seattle. Vested interests always oppose reforms that seem to threaten them. Our democratic advance has been slow because our people have been conservative. They have recognised that there has been much in established institutions that has been truly admirable, that rapid changes are apt to destroy more than they create, that there is an 'inevitability of gradualism' in more senses than one, and that they themselves have much to lose besides their chains. The outpourings of enthusiastic reformers must not be mistaken for the complaints of a frustrated people. If the people of this country want to overthrow capitalism, the public school system, the House of Lords or the monarchy, they have the power in their hands. If they have not done so, the explanation is that they have not wanted to do so. The monarchy, in fact, provides an excellent example. The Americans decided to overthrow monarchy nearly 200 years ago. It would be unnecessary now to use the methods that they then used: but since 1660 there has never been a really serious republican movement—certainly not since Joseph Chamberlain left the Liberal party. The stability of the monarchy does not depend on a condition imposed by a 'conciliatory upper class' in consideration of social reforms. It depends essentially on popular support.

The truth is that 'the most common and least privileged of the people' have generally been conservative, while the 'conciliatory upper class' has sometimes been, on American standards, quite radical. Thus arises the astonishing homogeneity of our political opinions, to which Bagehot drew attention and which the developments of a century have not affected. If it is necessary for democracy that the country should be rent by fierce conflict between the privileged and the under-privileged, we have not a democracy. But that kind of democracy is to be found neither in our books nor in our experience. Democracy, as we understand it, means that the people must be free, the free choose the rulers, and the rulers govern according to the wishes of the people.

INDEX

Administration
  bureaucracy in, 138–47
  civil service, 131–2, 135–6, *and see* Civil Service
  collection of information for, 134
  competition among Departments, 173–4
  conflicts of policy in, 174–8
  control of, 128
  co-ordination of, 167–9
  defence problems, 181–5
  Departments of, 131–2, 139–40, 168–9
  Departmental policy, 143, 179
  Departmental questions, 135
  duplication of functions, 171–3
  economic problems of, 186–93
  financial control of, 129, 179
  functions of, 126–30, 138
  inter-Departmental committees, 178–9
  methods of co-ordination, 178–93
  Ministers and, 132–3, *and see* Ministers
  overlapping of powers of, 170–1
  political questions and, 136–7
  process of, 131–38
  'red tape', 142
  Treasury control, 130, 178
Alternative vote, 20–1, 24–5
American colonies, coercion of, 38
Anti-Corn Law League, 6
'Appeasement', 144, 202
Asquith, H. H., Earl of Oxford and Asquith, 76, 116
Atlee, C. R., Earl Atlee, 118, 153, 190

Bagehot, Walter, 32
Baldwin, Stanley, Earl Baldwin of Bewdley, 113, 115, 158, 180, 187, 199, 200, 201
Balfour, A. J., Earl Balfour, 158, 164, 165
Bills, 85, *and see* House of Commons, House of Lords
Birkenhead, first Earl, 159
Birmingham Plan, 44–5
Bolingbroke, Viscount, 38, 204

Bonar Law, Andrew, 76, 115
British constitution,
  democracy, *see* Democracy
  empirical nature of, 125
  founded on land, 46
  historical defence of, 39
  'Old Corruption', 42–3, 45
  protected by Conservative party, 43
  simple principles of, 195
Bureaucracy, 138–47
Burke, Edmund, 38, 39
Butler, D. E., 71,
Butler, R. A., 116

Cabinet
  agenda, 154–5
  collective responsibility, 150–1
  committees of, 157
  composition of, 148–9
  decisions of, 135–6, 150–1
  Defence Committee, 181
  deficiencies of, 181–2
  generally, 151–62
  House of Commons matters in, 156
  inter-departmental conflicts, 155
  Legislation Committee, 92
  meetings of, 156
  party system and, 64
  policy-making by, 55–6, 174–8, 179–80
  public opinion and, 156
  Prime Minister and, 157
  secretariat of, 156–7, 187
  size of, 167–8
Cabinet Government
  generally, 148–93
  theory of, 134
Cabinet Office, 188
Campbell-Bannerman, Sir Henry, 158, 164
Carpet-baggers, 16
Caucus, 55–6
Central Statistical Office, 188, 191
Certiorari, order of 208
Chamberlain, Sir Austen, 162, 165
Chamberlain, Joseph, 1, 44–5, 47, 48, 49, 76, 155, 158, 159, 160, 162, 164, 165, 202, 203,

213